A GOOD YARN

A GOOD YARN

30 TIMELESS HATS,
SCARVES, SOCKS & GLOVES

KATHERINE POULTON

FOREWORD BY LILY COLE

A GOOD YARN

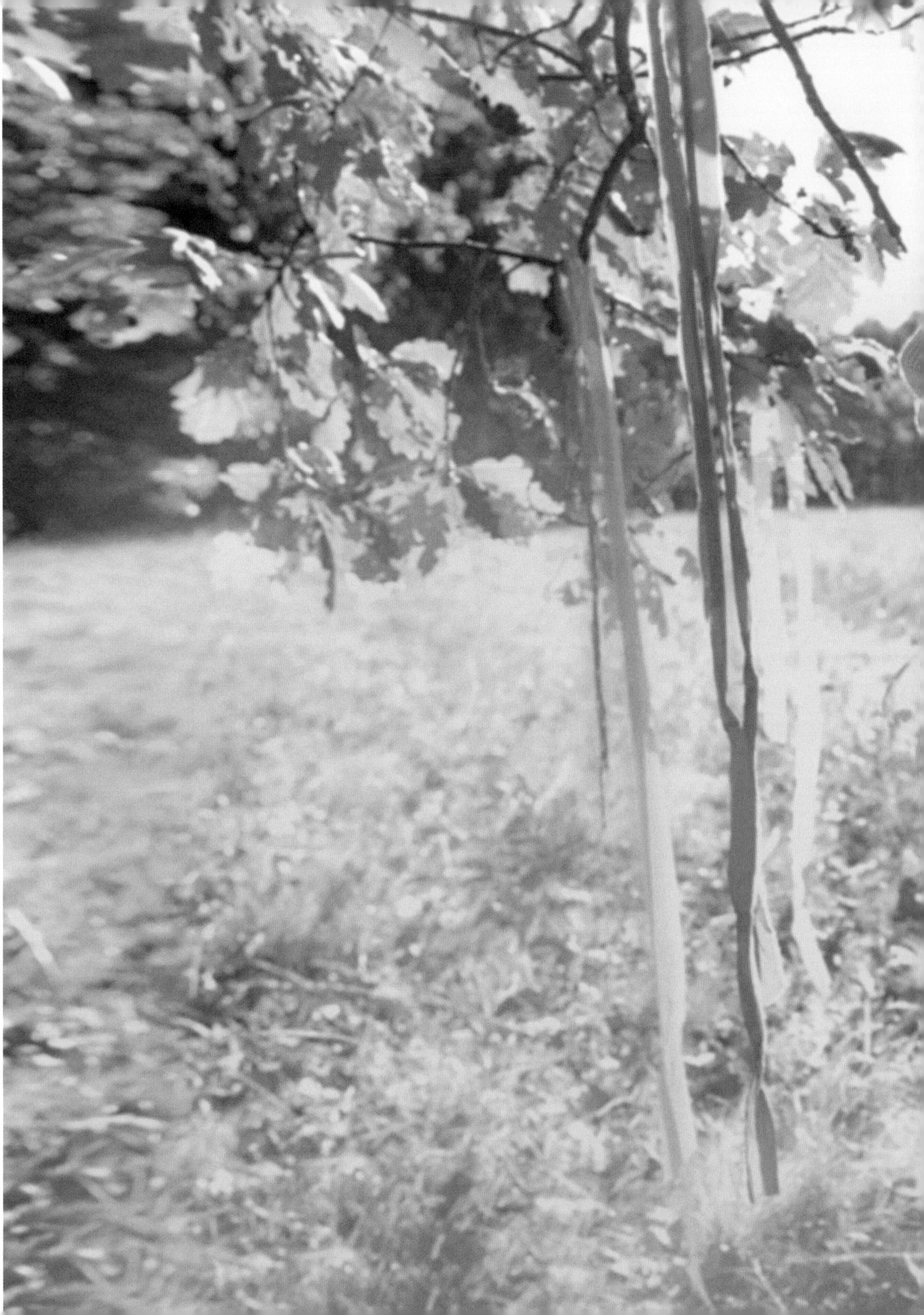

FOREWORD BY LILY COLE

Life in the fashion industry takes you from the inspiring and fantastical to the hard sell, with craftsmanship, skill and all that's woven in-between. We sought to bring our own flavour to the business. Something soulful and made with love.

We sought to connect the people who make, the producers, with the consumer. This has always been central to The North Circular's vision. I helped found The North Circular and continue to believe in it as a demonstration of transparency and sustainability. We believe in finding ways to prove that this is possible. That consumption can be humanised and non harmful, and most importantly, we can make desirable, practical knits that we love.

I spend my life trying to avoid patterns . . . well, patterns of behaviour that is. When it comes to knits I am a big fan of patterns. They imply a lineage that can be passed along and adapted over time. Originally, knitting patterns were passed on by word of mouth, through the generations within a family. They contain the secret formulae that can empower anyone - you or me or our grandmothers - to make something unique. Offering a logic to magic. A bit like recipes. A bit like spells.

Growing up having a grandma who knitted us jumpers was a real blessing. One year I went to Disneyland and I fell in love with a beautiful turquoise silk Princess Jasmine dress, but the high price tag meant I was reluctantly dragged past it by my family. That Christmas my grandma gave me a handmade version of the dress. I love the way the story behind an object infuses it; this idea has stayed with me. The energy that goes into making something infuses and becomes part of the finished item.

I truly believe if we were able to know and connect with the people involved in the processes of making and creating - whether by artisan hands or high-tech machines, whether it be a beanie or a Bentley - empathy and gratitude can shift our understanding of their value. The anonymity of capitalism, the opacity of objects' stories, arguably plays a large part in the social and environmental ills that production chains can so often be found to cause. So let's celebrate 'knit-ivism' and remind people that there is always a person behind everything, and that objects contain time, effort and work - and sometimes love and magic too.

Through The North Circular, we try to connect generations and share stories. To pass down our knitters' pearls and purls of wisdom, so that stories aren't lost and secrets are kept alive. We also create new patterns - new stories - informed by contemporary design and high fashion - so that the dialogue runs both ways . . . and so that we will have patterns, knits, purls and pearls - new and old - to pass on to our children.

INTRODUCTION

Starting The North Circular knitwear line, we were inspired by the idea that everyone could be connected to what they wore; everyone could be clothed in something made with love, something they would value and look after – connected not only to the person who made it, but also to the knitting traditions that have been handed down through generations. We aim to celebrate the 'grannies, girls and a few strong men' that knit for us, introducing them by name on each knitted piece they make. These traditional skills of knitting and the passing on of knowledge from experienced knitter to beginner can continue even into our machine age. In the same way that we connect our customers to the knitters who made their pieces, we want to connect all aspiring knitters to learn and share with each other and pass on their skills and wisdom.

We first conceived the idea for The North Circular in 2009, and with it aimed to offer a key to a brighter, warmer future. We were looking to provoke thought and spread some warm fuzzy feelings with the simplest knits. Global markets were entering a recession, but we stayed true to our beliefs and said maybe we could make it – and make it here. Maybe our homespun talents are hiding in your knitting basket; maybe we can create beautiful yarns from our animals without shipping anything around the world. Maybe the customer on the shop floor would like to trace it all back, and think that someone's hands made these pieces, that the animal whose fleece they were wearing lives on England's green pastures, saw the same rain they saw . . . appreciate that local jobs – farming, spinning, dyeing, knitting, making – were supported.

Armed with our fashion background, lustrous yarns and a tight colour palette, we wanted to inspire people to think about where their clothes came from – not just the finished piece itself, but the elements that made it up – the fibre, the effort, the skill involved in making their knits, the person behind the talent, with the knitter's name labelled on each individual piece. Educated with the alternatives, people can use their consumer power to choose, buying into a way to change the world, one purchase at a time.

We took the best pure natural yarns we could find locally – Wensleydale and Blue-faced Leicester wools, alpaca and British cashmere. Brimming with these ideas, we created a new model for how we wanted our manufacturing done. The cornerstone of the concept was handmade, which threw us into the deep end with the question: How can you individually hand make a luxury item and retail it to the biggest names in fashion on a mass scale?

It seemed impossible, and we are still learning, but with beginners' enthusiasm and naivety, we loved the idea so much it had to have a chance at life. The first season we launched, international retail orders poured in, closely followed by full-page spreads in the September issue of *Vogue* and other key magazines. We were beside ourselves with joy, until the grand scale of the operation we were about to embark upon dawned on us. Dreams coming true are only the start of the story, with the highs and lows of running a fledgling business making the dream very real indeed.

We committed to the idea that not only would the person who bought our knits have something made with love, it would be natural, procured from the earth and able to go back into the earth at the end of its life cycle, and one day grow again. With these beliefs firmly guiding the production methods, all of our combined experiences absorbed from the fashion houses and photography studios of the world as models fed into the aesthetic we created. We wanted people to get a feel-good local product with a great philosophy, but with the style and feel that they desired from a great quality product.

But we know the customer will only buy such a product because they desire it, love the style and feel and recognise the quality. Although the seasons of fashion change and hemlines rise and fall, we aimed for our look to be style rather than fashion – luxury basics with a twist that you can work into every outfit, timeless classics that you can wear until the wheels fall off, someone pinches your lovely hat or one glove disappears!

It's a big spiral upwards from cottage industry to industrial revolution and on again, but we were excited to accept the challenge. So, with a lot of good advice and managing to take some of it on board, we have established The North Circular as the place to buy luxury handmade goods and the best beanies in town, which are marketed globally and sold worldwide.

We are excited for you to get creating, learning, sharing and wearing our styles knitted in your own style. We do love a good yarn, but we'll shut up now and let you get on with exploring our patterns . . .

'I think we are all so increasingly obsessed and addicted to the new (myself included) that there's a real danger of us forgetting to look back, appreciate, and hold on to the amazing things, values, skills and traditions that previous generations and the past offer us. I'm really interested in marrying the old and the new, allowing them to coexist, enhance and inform one another – whether it's reading about sufism on my iPad, or wearing a modern, sleek, designed hat hand knitted, old-school style in real wool!'
LILY COLE

THE PATTERNS

CLASSIC BOBBLE

BOBBLE (*noun*) a small ball made of strands of wool used as a decoration on a hat.

A frivolous creation, a bobble is a soft globe of yarn whose only function in life is to create a soundless bobbing motion on top of your head. It also breaks the hard edges of life, tempering sensible outfits back to the meaning of winter dressing, and cheers you up, so you can push on through. And that, of course, is how you make a bobble, pushing yarn through, again and again, never ceasing until, shorn and tightly belted like a 1950s pin-up, it is released from the restrictions that created it, and fills out and blooms. Here we've added the latest colour blocking and a luxuriously generous bobble to give cartoon-like proportions to this iconic hat style.

MEASUREMENTS
29cm from bottom edge to crown
14cm deep rib
23cm wide, sewn up

YARN
250g Aran yarn, 1 strand

TENSION
10cm square in stocking stitch: 15 sts x 19 rows

NEEDLES AND NOTIONS
5mm knitting needles
Tapestry needle
Card to make pompom template

STITCHES AND TECHNIQUES
2 x 2 rib
Stocking stitch
Pompom

INSTRUCTIONS

Cast on 74 sts, leaving 80cm end of yarn for sewing up.

2 x 2 rib
Row 1 (RS): *P2, K2, repeat from * to last 2 sts, P2.
Row 2: *K2, P2, repeat from * to last 2 sts, K2.
Repeat these 2 rows 12 more times. 26 rows completed.

Stocking stitch crown
Row 27: K.
Row 28: P.
Repeat these 2 rows 7 more times. 42 rows completed.

Shape crown
Row 43: K1, *K6, K2tog, repeat from * to last st, K1.

Row 44 and all alternate rows: P.
Row 45: K1, *K5, K2tog, repeat from * to last st, K1.
Row 47: K1, *K4, K2tog, repeat from * to last st, K1.
Row 49: K1, *K3, K2tog, repeat from * to last st, K1.
Row 51: K1, *K2, K2tog, repeat from * to last st, K1.
Row 53: K1, *K1, K2tog, repeat from * to last st, K1.
Row 55: K1, *K2tog, repeat from * to last st, K1. 11 sts.
Row 56: *P2tog, repeat from * to last st, P1. 6 sts.

TO MAKE UP
Cut off the yarn, leaving a long end. Using the
tapestry needle, thread yarn through the remaining
stitches and pull tightly, avoiding puckering. Sew in
the end, securing the stitches.

Starting on the wrong side (for the rib will be turned
wrong side out later), sew the rib edges together
two-thirds of the way up (about 9cm) from the cast-
on edge. Turn to the right side and continue stitching
to the top of the crown.

Cut out two pompom templates from card. They
should be 10cm in diameter with a 2.5cm hole. Make
a pompom, tying the centre tightly, and fasten it on
top of the hat. Sew in the loose ends.

TOMLIN SCARF

This traditional, long weighty scarf is a reminder of when winters were winters and scarves were lifesavers. Accidental rib used for this scarf gives a loose, open texture and is great for men and women. The bright red used here is bound to brighten everyone's grey days. Generous fringing may not save you from freezing – but perhaps from being taken too seriously.

MEASUREMENTS, LYING FLAT SEWN UP
Scarf: 175cm long x 20cm wide
Fringe: 17cm long

YARN
600g DK yarn, 2 strands together 500g in red
(MC) and 100g in slate (CC)

TENSION
10cm square in accidental rib, measured relaxed:
22 sts x 22 rows

NEEDLES AND NOTIONS
6mm knitting needles
Tapestry needle

STITCHES AND TECHNIQUES
Accidental rib

INSTRUCTIONS

Cast on 47 sts in MC.
Row 1: *K2, P2, repeat from * to last 3 sts, K3.
Repeat row 1 to create accidental rib pattern.
Continue for 175cm. Cast off loosely in rib or using a
crochet cast off method.

TO MAKE UP
Sew all the ends into the centre of the scarf rather
than along the outer edge.

The fringe is made of strands of CC yarn cut into
lengths of 34cm. There are two strands of yarn in
each tassel. Between 39 and 41 tassels are needed to
form each fringe.

Pass two strands of cut yarn up through one end
stitch on the scarf and back through the next end
stitch, leaving a loop. Pass all four strand ends
through the loop and pull to secure a chunky knot.
Continue to add tassels evenly along both ends of the
scarf, with all the knots on the same side.

'Even if the phone's ringing, the
doorbell's going and the pan's boiling
over, always finish your row first!'
GRAN EILEEN

CHUNKY STRIPE HAT

We love this hat in navy and natural to give nautical stripes, or with jet and navy stripes for a more masculine look. But this is really the place for your imagination to bring in your favourite colour scheme. The hat is oversized, giving scope for pulling the back down into a slouchy look.This humble beanie has graced the pages of *Teen Vogue* in these nautical stripes. When it featured in British *Vogue* in chunky wool plain knit, the model liked it so much she kept it. So watch out – once you've put all your love into it, it's an irresistible hat!

MEASUREMENTS

30cm from bottom edge to crown

13cm deep rib

24.5cm wide, sewn up

YARN

130g Aran yarn, 1 strand, 65g in natural (MC) and 65g in navy (CC)

TENSION

10cm square in stocking stitch: 14 sts x 19 rows

NEEDLES AND NOTIONS

6mm knitting needles

Tapestry needle

STITCHES AND TECHNIQUES

2 x 2 rib

Stocking stitch

INSTRUCTIONS

Cast on 78 sts in MC, leaving 80cm end of yarn for sewing up.

2 x 2 rib

Row 1 (RS): *K2, P2, repeat from * to last 2 sts, K2.

Row 2: *P2, K2, repeat from * to last 2 sts, P2.

Repeat these two rows 2 more times (6 rows in total). Change to CC and work a further 6 rows in rib. Continue in rib for 24 rows in total, changing colour every 6 rows.

Stocking stitch crown

Work 18 rows in st st, changing colour every 6 rows as before.

Shape crown

Row 43: K1, [K7, K2tog] twice, K to last 12 sts, K2tog, K7, K2tog, K1.

Row 44 and all alternate rows: P.

Row 45: K1, *K6, K2tog, repeat from * to last st, K1.

Row 47: K1, *K5, K2tog, repeat from * to last st, K1.

Row 49: K1, *K4, K2tog, repeat from * to last st, K1.

Row 51: K1, *K3, K2tog, repeat from * to last st, K1.

Row 53: K1, *K2, K2tog, repeat from * to last st, K1.

Row 55: K1, *K1, K2tog, repeat from * to last st, K1.

Row 57: K1, *K2tog, repeat from * to last st, K1. 11 sts.

Row 59: K1, *K2tog, repeat from * to end. 6 sts.

TO MAKE UP

Cut off the yarn, leaving a long end. Using the tapestry needle, thread yarn through the remaining stitches and pull tightly, avoiding puckering. Sew in the end, securing the stitches.

Taking care to match the stripes, fold in half and sew the edges together from the bottom of the rib to the top of the crown. Sew in the loose ends.

TWIST SNOOD HOOD

Walking the musty corridors of London's museums, there are glass cabinets filled with war-beaten metals, chain mail, gauntlets and helmets – hand-crafted metals worn to protect the body in challenging battles of times gone by. We took our silvery grey yarn to echo the beaten armour and our sturdy but stretchy twisted rib stitch to hold the hooded shape for an altogether different confrontation field – modern life. There are three ways to wear this versatile hood – as a long snood, twisted once over the head with the hood up and also flattened with one end passed through the loop in the other end.

MEASUREMENTS

186cm long all round x 22cm wide

YARN

460g DK yarns, 2 strands together

TENSION

10cm square in twisted rib, measured relaxed:
23 sts x 20 rows

NEEDLES AND NOTIONS

5mm knitting needles
Tapestry needle

STITCHES AND TECHNIQUES

1 x 1 twisted rib

INSTRUCTIONS

Cast on 58 sts.
Row 1: K2, *KB1, P1, repeat from * to last 2 sts, K2.
Row 2: P2, *K1, PB1, repeat from * to last 2 sts, P2.
Repeat these two rows until work measures about
83cm.

Shape hood

Continue working in 1 x 1 twisted rib.
With RS facing, and counting next row as row 1, dec 1
st at right-hand edge only on rows 1, 4, 7, 9, 11, 13, 15,
16, 17, 18, 19, 20, 21, 22. 44 sts.
Now, counting next row as row 1 again, inc 1 st at the
same edge on rows 1, 2, 3, 4, 5, 6, 7, 8, 10, 12, 14, 16,
19, 22. 58 sts.
Continue twisted rib on these 58 sts for further
83cm. Cast off in rib.

TO MAKE UP

Fold the scarf in half, placing the cast-on and cast-off
edges together. If one of the edges is wider than the
other, run the attached length of yarn through the
end stitches and pull the edge up so it is the same
width as the other edge. This helps the seam to lie
flat. Sew the ends together.

Sew the hood's curved edges together, starting at the
top and continuing around the curve for about 33cm
to create the hood.

Use a single strand of yarn to sew up where multiple
strands have been used in the knitting to avoid bulky
seams.

AARON GLOVES

Aran knitting comes from the rocky islands near Galway Bay off the west coast of Ireland. Now world-renowned for intricate cables, these chunky textured patterns were originally conceived by the island women to clothe their men. Knitted in pure Aran wool, which is rich in natural lanolin, the garments are wind and weatherproof. Handed down through the generations from mother to daughter, intricate Aran patterns are now written down for all to try. Many of our designs are inspired by Aran stitches. Here we have translated a graphic Aran pattern made up of twisted rib, with moss stitch zigzagging across opposing diagonals, to create symmetry for this pair of gloves. A simple thumb hole and open fingers make these perfect, simple gloves.

'NOTHING IS FOOL PROOF, BE WELL PREPARED, READ AND RE-READ THE PATTERN, KNIT YOUR TENSION SQUARE AND DO YOURSELF A FAVOUR BY GETTING THE RIGHT YARN FOR THE PATTERN - OR YOU MAY BE LOOKING FOR SOMEONE WITH BIG HANDS TO GIVE YOUR GLOVES TOO!'
SHEILA NICHOLS

MEASUREMENTS
28cm long x 9cm wide

YARN
100g DK yarn, 1 strand

TENSION
10cm square in stocking stitch: 20 sts x 24 rows

NEEDLES AND NOTIONS
4mm knitting needles
Cable needle
Tapestry needle

STITCHES AND TECHNIQUES
1 x 1 twisted rib
Half-diamond pattern
Stocking stitch
Double moss stitch
Cabling

SPECIAL ABBREVIATIONS
C1f slip next stitch to cable needle, leave at front of work, knit 1 (or purl 1 as appropriate to pattern) from left-hand needle, then KB1 from cable needle
C1b slip next stitch to cable needle, leave at back of work, KB1 from left-hand needle, then knit 1 (or purl 1 as appropriate to pattern) from cable needle

INSTRUCTIONS

RIGHT GLOVE
Cast on 38 sts, leaving long end of yarn for sewing up.

1 x 1 twisted rib
Row 1: *KB1, P1, repeat from * to end.
Row 2: *K1, PB1, repeat from * to end.
Repeat these two rows 8 times (16 rows in total).

The following pattern is for half-diamond panel only. Work 20 sts in st st for the palm, then 18 sts in half-diamond pattern for the back of the glove:e.g.
Row 1: K20; [KB1, P1] 5 times, KB1, [P1, K1] 3 times, P1.

Half-diamond pattern
Row 1(RS): [KB1, P1] 5 times, KB1, [P1, K1] 3 times, P1.
Row 2: [K1, P1] 3 times, K1, [PB1, K1] 5 times, PB1.
Row 3: [KB1, P1] 3 times, [C1f] 3 times, [P1, K1] 3 times.
Row 4: [P1, K1] 3 times, [PB1, K1] twice, PB2, [K1, PB1] 3 times.
Row 5: [KB1, P1] 3 times, KB1, [C1f] 3 times, [P1, K1] twice, P1.
Row 6: [K1, P1] twice, K1, [PB1, K1] 6 times, PB1.
Row 7: [KB1, P1] 4 times, [C1f] 3 times, [P1, K1] twice.
Row 8: [P1, K1] twice, [PB1, K1] twice, PB2, [K1, PB1] 4 times.
Row 9: [KB1, P1] 4 times, KB1, [C1f] 3 times, P1, K1, P1.
Row 10: K1, P1, K1, [PB1, K1] 7 times, PB1.
Row 11: [KB1, P1] 5 times, [C1f] 3 times, P1, K1.
Row 12: P1, K1, [PB1, K1] twice, PB2, [K1, PB1] 5 times.
Row 13: [KB1, P1] 5 times, KB1, [C1f] 3 times, P1.
Row 14: [K1, PB1] 9 times.

Row 15: [KB1, P1] 6 times, [C1f] 3 times.

Row 16: [PB1, K1] twice, PB2, [K1, PB1] 6 times.

Row 17: [KB1, P1] 6 times, [C1b] 3 times.

Row 18: [K1, PB1] 9 times.

Row 19: [KB1, P1] 5 times, KB1, [C1b] 3 times, K1.

Row 20: P1, K1, [PB1, K1] twice, PB2, [K1, PB1] 5 times.

Row 21: [KB1, P1] 5 times, [C1b] 3 times, K1, P1.

Row 22: K1, P1, K1, [PB1, K1] 7 times, PB1.

Row 23: [KB1, P1] 4 times, KB1, [C1b] 3 times, K1, P1, K1.

Row 24: [P1, K1] twice, [PB1, K1] twice, PB2, [K1, PB1] 4 times.

Row 25: [KB1, P1] 4 times, [C1b] 3 times, [K1, P1] twice.

Row 26: [K1, P1] twice, K1, [PB1, K1] 6 times, PB1.

Row 27: [KB1, P1] 3 times, KB1, [C1b] 3 times, [K1, P1] twice, K1.

Row 28: [P1, K1] 3 times, [PB1, K1] twice, PB2, [K1, PB1] 3 times.

Row 29: [KB1, P1] 3 times, [C1b] 3 times, [K1, P1] 3 times.

Row 30: [K1, P1] 3 times, [K1, PB1] 6 times.
Row 31: [KB1, P1] twice, KB1, [C1b] 3 times, [K1, P1] 3 times, K1.
Row 32: [P1, K1] 4 times, [PB1, K1] twice, PB2, [K1, PB1] twice.
Row 33: [KB1, P1] twice, [C1b] 3 times, [K1, P1] 4 times.
Row 34: [K1, P1] 4 times, [K1, PB1] 5 times.
Row 35: KB1, P1, KB1, [C1b] 3 times, [K1, P1] 4 times, K1.
Row 36: [P1, K1] 5 times, [PB1, K1] twice, PB2, K1, PB1.
Row 37: KB1, P1, [C1b] 3 times, [K1, P1] 5 times.
Row 38: [K1, P1] 5 times, K1, [PB1, K1] 3 times, PB1.
Row 39: KB1, [C1b] 3 times, [K1, P1] 5 times, K1.
Row 40: [P1, K1] 6 times, [PB1, K1] twice, PB2.
Row 41: KB1, [C1f] 3 times, [P1, K1] 5 times, P1.
Row 42: [K1, P1] 5 times, K1, [PB1, K1] 3 times, PB1.
Row 43: KB1, P1, [C1f] 3 times, [P1, K1] 5 times.
Row 44: [P1, K1] 5 times, [PB1, K1] twice, PB2, K1, PB1.
Row 45: KB1, P1, KB1, [C1f] 3 times, [P1, K1] 4 times, P1.
Row 46: [K1, P1] 4 times, K1, [PB1, K1] 4 times, PB1.
Row 47: [KB1, P1] twice, [C1f] 3 times, [P1, K1] 4 times.
Row 48: [P1, K1] 4 times, [PB1, K1] twice, PB2, [K1, PB1] twice.
Row 49: [KB1, P1] twice, KB1, [C1f] 3 times, [P1, K1] 3 times, P1.
Row 50: [K1, P1] 3 times, K1, [PB1, K1] 5 times, PB1.

Work further 8 rows in 1 x 1 twisted rib.
Cast off in rib, leaving end of yarn long enough to stitch together the finger end rib.

LEFT GLOVE

Cast on as for right glove and work 1 x 1 twisted rib as follows:
Row 1: *P1, KB1, repeat from * to end.
Row 2: *PB1, K1, repeat from * to end.
Repeat these two rows 8 times (16 rows in total).

To form left hand panel with diamond facing in the opposite direction, read the rows from end to beginning and work the reverse twist for moved stitches, reading C1f for C1b and C1b for C1f; then work 20 sts in st st for the palm, e.g.
Row 1: P1, [K1, P1] 3 times, KB1, [P1, KB1] 5 times; K20.

Work further 8 rows in 1 x 1 twisted rib.
Cast off in rib, leaving end of yarn long enough to stitch together the finger end rib.

TO MAKE UP

Fold in half with right sides facing. Sew the side edges together, from the cast off edge to the top of the thumb opening (about 4cm) and from the cast on edge upwards, leaving a 5cm hole for the thumb. Sew in the loose ends.

RIB BEANIE

Ribbing. It's always functional as it stretches out around your head like a musical organ, securing the hat so it hangings on tightly through wind and rain. This is the ultimate British summer weather accessory. The wool has the unique quality of holding in heat in both dry and wet weather, which means you can meet the elements head on.

'DO YOU MIND IF I BANG ON ABOUT KNOTS?! KNOTS SHOULD NEVER FEATURE IN A HAND-KNITTED GARMENT. WOOL SHOULD BE JOINED AT THE BEGINNING OF A ROW AND THE RESULTING ENDS SEWN INTO THE SEAM. ON THE VERY RARE OCCASIONS WHEN A KNOT IS NECESSARY IN THE MIDDLE OF KNITTING, I.E. WHEN A THREAD IN THE YARN HAS BEEN KNOTTED DURING MANUFACTURE AND APPEARS UNSAFE, THEN CUT THE WOOL AND REJOIN BY PUTTING THE TWO ENDS SIDE-BY-SIDE AND KNITTING THE NEXT THREE STITCHES WITH THE TWO ENDS, TIDY THE TWO ENDS BY SEWING NEATLY INTO THE BACK OF THE STITCHES. OR YOU CAN ALWAYS UNPICK THE ROW AND EMPLOY THE FIRST METHOD.'
SHIRLEY

MEASUREMENTS

29.5cm from bottom edge to crown

15cm wide when unstretched and folded in half

YARN

200g Aran yarn, 1 strand

TENSION

10cm square in 2 x 2 rib, measured relaxed: 23 sts x 19 rows

NEEDLES AND NOTIONS

5mm knitting needles

Tapestry needle

STITCHES AND TECHNIQUES

2 x 2 rib

INSTRUCTIONS

Cast on 82 sts, leaving 80cm end of yarn for sewing up.

2 x 2 rib

Row 1 (RS): *K2, P2, repeat from * to last 2 sts, K2.

Row 2: *P2, K2, repeat from * to last 2 sts, P2.

Repeat rows 1 and 2 until 44 rows are completed.

Shape crown

Row 45: K1, *K1, P2, K2, P1, K2tog, repeat from * to last st, K1.

Row 46 and all alternate rows: K knit sts and P purl sts, ensuring to purl K2tog st from previous row.

Row 47: K1, *K1, P2, K2, K2tog, repeat from * to last st, K1.

Row 49: K1, *K1, P2, K1, K2tog, repeat from * to last st, K1.

Row 51: K1, *K1, P2, K2tog, repeat from * to last st, K1.

Row 53: K1, *K1, P1, K2tog, repeat from * to last st, K1.

Row 55: K1, *K1, K2tog, repeat from * to last st, K1.

Row 57: K1, *K2tog, repeat from * to last st, K1. 12 sts.

Row 58: P1, *P2tog, repeat from * to last st, P1. 7 sts.

TO MAKE UP

Break off the yarn, leaving a long end. Using the tapestry needle, thread the yarn through the remaining stitches and pull tightly, ensuring that the work does not pucker. Sew in the end, securing the stitches.

Starting on the wrong side (for the bottom part of the rib will be turned wrong side out later), sew the edges together, about 9cm up from the cast-on edge. Turn to the right side and continue stitching to the top of the crown. Sew in the loose ends.

BYKER GLOVES

Beaten-up, tight-fitting, cut-off leather biker gloves that have seen many a road trip inspired these hand-hugging gloves. The tiny moss stitch banding in jet black holds the hand securely, while the contrasting grey of the half fingers and cuffs ties into the latest colour-blocking styles. The cuffs are worked in 2 x 2 rib, while moss stitch across the hand gives the rugged look and stocking stitch ensures the fingers and thumb have plenty of mobility.

MEASUREMENTS
21cm long x 11cm wide

YARN
70g 3-ply yarn, 1 strand, 35g in black (MC), 35g in grey (CC)

TENSION
10cm square in moss stitch: 28 sts x 46 rows

NEEDLES AND NOTIONS
Set of 2.25mm double-pointed knitting needles
Place marker
Tapestry needle

STITCHES AND TECHNIQUES
Moss stitch
Stocking stitch
2 x 2 rib
Circular knitting

NOTES
Keep the moss stitches firm.
The **M1** increase is made by knitting into the front, then the back of the st.

INSTRUCTIONS

RIGHT GLOVE
Using CC, cast on 48 sts. Divide sts between 3 DPNs. Join, being careful not to twist cast-on row sts. PM at beginning of round.

2 x 2 rib
Work 2 x 2 rib (K2, P2) for 34 rounds.
Using MC, change to moss st as follows:
Round 1: *K1, P1, repeat from * to end of round.
Round 2: *P1, K1, repeat from * to end of round.
Repeat rounds 1 and 2 five times (10 rounds in total).

Shape thumb gusset
Moss st continues, but thumb gusset is worked in st st.
Round 1: [K1, P1] 12 times, M1, K1, M1, [P1, K1] 10 times, P1.
Rounds 2 and 4: [P1, K1] 12 times, K5, [K1, P1] 10 times, K1.
Round 3: [K1, P1] 12 times, K5, [P1, K1] 10 times, P1.
Round 5: [K1, P1] 12 times, M1, K3, M1, [P1, K1] 10 times, P1.
Rounds 6 and 8: [P1, K1] 12 times, K7, [K1, P1] 10 times, K1.
Round 7: [K1, P1] 12 times, K7, [P1, K1] 10 times, P1.
Round 9: [K1, P1] 12 times, M1, K5, M1, [P1, K1] 10 times, P1.
Rounds 10 and 12: [P1, K1] 12 times, K9, [K1, P1] 10 times, K1.
Round 11: [K1, P1] 12 times, K9, [P1, K1] 10 times, P1.
Continue working in this manner, inc (M1) 1 st on each side of gusset every 4th round, until there are 60 sts on needle. Work 3 more rounds without shaping.
Round 25: [K1, P1] 12 times, sl next 15 sts onto length of yarn (for thumb), cast on 3 sts, [P1, K1] 10 times, P1.
Work 21 more rounds in moss st (22 rounds after thumb gusset in total).

First finger
All fingers are worked in st st using CC.
Round 1: K6, slip all but last 5 sts onto holding yarn, cast on 2 sts, K5. Divide sts onto 3 DPNs. 13 sts.
Knit 11 more rounds (12 rounds in total).
Cast off fairly loosely for flexible edge. Break off yarn. With tapestry needle, sew in end making sure to complete cast-off 'chain' for a neat look.

Second finger
Round 1: Join yarn. K6 from holding yarn, cast on 2

sts, K last 6 sts from holding yarn, pick up and K2 from base of first finger. Divide sts onto 3 DPNs. 16 sts.
Knit 13 more rounds (14 rounds in total).
Cast off and finish as first finger.

Third finger

Work and finish as second finger, but knit 15 rounds in total.

Fourth finger

Round 1: Join yarn. K13 from holding yarn, pick up and K3 from base of third finger. 16 sts.
Work and finish as second finger.

Thumb

Round 1: Join yarn. K15 from holding yarn, pick up and K3 from base of hand. Divide sts onto 3 DPNs. 18 sts.
Work 12 more rounds (13 rounds in total). Finish as fingers.

LEFT GLOVE

Work cuff as for right glove. Change to moss st and work 10 rounds as for right glove.

Shape thumb gusset (in reverse)

Round 1: [K1, P1] 10 times, K1, M1, K1, M1, [K1, P1] 12 times.
Rounds 2 and 4: [P1, K1] 10 times, P1, K5, [P1, K1] 12 times.
Round 3: [K1, P1] 10 times, K1, K5, [K1, P1] 12 times.
Round 5: [K1, P1] 10 times, K1, M1, K3, M1, [K1, P1] 12 times.
Rounds 6 and 8: [P1, K1] 10 times, P1, K7, [P1, K1] 12 times.
Round 7: [K1, P1] 10 times, K1, K7, [K1, P1] 12 times.
Round 9: [K1, P1] 10 times, K1, M1, K5, M1, [K1, P1] 12 times.

Rounds 10 and 12: [P1, K1] 10 times, P1, K9, [P1, K1] 12 times.
Round 11: [K1, P1] 10 times, K1, K9, [K1, P1] 12 times.
Continue working in this manner, inc (M1) 1 st on each side of gusset every 4th round, until there are 60 sts on needle. Work 3 more rounds without shaping.
Round 25: [K1, P1] 10 times, K1, sl next 15 sts onto length of yarn (for thumb), cast on 3 sts, [K1, P1] 12 times.
Work 21 more rounds in moss st (22 rounds after thumb gusset in total).
Work rest of glove as right glove.

TO MAKE UP

Sew in all the remaining ends at the bottom of all the fingers, making sure to close up any gaps left after casting on between the fingers.

SEA SCARF

The long twisting cables on this scarf echo the waves of the ocean and cumulate in an equilateral triangle, inspired by the masonic carvings in the curb stones of London's ancient streets, which we still walk upon today. The triangle is found in every culture – being symmetrical and mathematically perfect, it is often used as a symbol for deity, a perfect being.

'HAIRGRIPS ARE MY SECRET TOOL. WHEN I'M HOLDING A SMALL NUMBER OF STITCHES, I USE MY HAIRGRIPS TO HOLD THEM IN PLACE. AND WHEN I'M FRINGING A SCARF, AS I CAST ON I PUT A HAIRGRIP IN EACH STITCH. THEN IT'S EASY TO FIND THE RIGHT STITCH TO PUT THE FRINGE IN PLACE.'
CAROLE CARR

MEASUREMENTS
Scarf: 173cm long x 22cm wide
Fringe: 17cm long

YARN
800g Aran yarn, 1 strand

TENSION
10cm square in stocking stitch: 14 sts x 19 rows

NEEDLES AND NOTIONS
6mm knitting needles
Cable needle
Tapestry needle

STITCHES AND TECHNIQUES
Garter stitch
Cabling
Moss stitch

NOTES
The cable pattern is shown between ( ).
Remember to knit crossed stitches while twisting 3 back (T3B) or front (T3F).

INSTRUCTIONS

Cast on 32 sts and knit 2 rows.

Triangle pattern
Row 1: (RS) and all odd rows: P1, K1, P1, K26, P1, K1, P1.
Row 2: P1, K1, P1, K12, P2, K12, P1, K1, P1.
Row 4: P1, K1, P1, K11, P4, K11, P1, K1, P1.
Row 6: P1, K1, P1, K10, P6, K10, P1, K1, P1.
Row 8: P1, K1, P1, K9, P8, K9, P1, K1, P1.
Row 10: P1, K1, P1, K8, P10, K8, P1, K1, P1.
Row 12: P1, K1, P1, K7, P12, K7, P1, K1, P1.
Row 14: P1, K1, P1, K6, P14, K6, P1, K1, P1.
Row 16: P1, K1, P1, K5, P16, K5, P1, K1, P1.

Cable pattern
Row 1 (RS): P1, K1, P1, K26, P1, K1, P1.
Row 2: P1, K1, P1, K5, (P2, K4, P4, K4, P2), K5, P1, K1, P1.
Row 3: P1, K1, P1, K5, (K6, C4B, K6), K5, P1, K1, P1.
Row 4: As row 2.
Row 5: P1, K1, P1, K5, ([T3F, K2, T3B] twice), K5, P1, K1, P1.
Row 6: P1, K1, P1, K5, (K1, [P2, K2] 3 times, P2, K1), K5, P1, K1, P1.
Row 7: P1, K1, P1, K5, (K1, T3F, T3B, K2, T3F, T3B, K1), K5, P1, K1, P1.
Row 8: P1, K1, P1, K5, (K2, P4, K4, P4, K2), K5, P1, K1, P1.
Row 9: P1, K1, P1, K5, (K2, C4B, K4, C4B, K2), K5, P1, K1, P1.
Row 10: As row 8.
Row 11: As row 1.
Rows 12 and 13: As rows 8 and 9.
Row 14: As row 8.
Row 15: P1, K1, P1, K5 (K1, T3B, T3F, K2, T3B, T3F, K1), K5, P1, K1, P1.
Row 16: As row 6.
Row 17: P1, K1, P1, K5, ([T3B, K2, T3F] twice), K5, P1, K1, P1.
Rows 18 and 19: As rows 2 and 3.
Row 20: As row 2.
Repeat rows 1–20 fifteen more times. (16 double crossover cable repeats in total.)
Repeat row 1 once more.

Triangle pattern
Create triangle at end by working triangle pattern in reverse, from row 16 to row 1. Knit 2 rows and cast off.

TO MAKE UP

Sew all the ends into the centre of the scarf rather than along the outer edge.

The fringe is made of strands of yarn cut into lengths of 38cm. There are four strands of yarn in each tassel. Create 11 tassels along each end of the scarf.

Pass four strands of cut yarn up through one end stitch on the scarf and back through the next end stitch, leaving a loop. Pass all eight strand ends through the loop and pull to secure a chunky knot. Continue to add tassels evenly along both ends of the scarf, ensuring that all the knots are on the same side.

Alternatively use finer yarn with more strands per tassel.

EARHART COLLAR

Amelia Earhart, the glamorous female aviatrix, was one of the early aircraft pioneers, and the first woman to fly solo over the Atlantic and Pacific oceans. The exhilarating freedom and danger that the skies represented in the 1920s and 30s are hard to imagine now. In 1937, Amelia mysteriously disappeared whilst attempting to fly around the world, leaving only the iconic imagery of her in her flying regalia. Wrapping up against the coldest of skies, early aviation gear consisted of functional shearing caps and coats. The chunky, textured Earhart Collar, worn with the shaped Aviator Hat, is our interpretation of aviation gear.

MEASUREMENTS

62cm long all round

25cm deep at back

12cm deep at front

YARN

500g Aran yarn, 2 strands together

TENSION

10cm square in moss stitch: 9 sts x 16 rows

NEEDLES AND NOTIONS

9mm knitting needles

Tapestry needle

STITCHES AND TECHNIQUES

Moss stitch

NOTES

Make sure the front join on the collar is extra secure as it takes all the strain when pulled over the head.

INSTRUCTIONS

Cast on 55 sts, leaving long end of yarn for sewing up.

Work in moss st as follows:

Row 1: *K1, P1, repeat from* to last st, K1.

Repeat this row 22 times in total.

Shape collar

Dec 1 st (work first st, K2tog/P2tog in pattern; K2tog/P2tog in pattern, work last st) on each edge of rows 23, 26, 29, 31, 33, 35, 37, 38, 39, 40 and 41. 33 sts.

Inc 1 st (work first st, M1; M1, work last st) on each edge of rows 43, 44, 45, 46, 47, 49, 51, 53, 55, 58, 61. 55 sts.

Work 22 more rows in moss st without shaping.

Cast off.

TO MAKE UP

Fold the collar in half lengthways, then place the cast-on and cast-off edges together, then double up by folding top to bottom. Using single yarn to avoid a bulky seam, neatly sew these edges together on the outside of the garment.

With the cast-on and cast-off edges at the bottom, sew the side edges together from the bottom edge for about 12cm to the beginning of the collar shaping. Make sure the neck join is secure by sewing in any long ends.

'There's an integrity and something wonderfully holistic about the world of knit – which is made all the more accessible and enticing since The North Circular got hold of it.'
JESSICA BUMPUS, VOGUE.COM

AVIATOR HAT

Inspired by the great female aviation pioneers, this close-fitting feminine hat is designed to frame the face. It also provides an easy way to practise increasing and decreasing to give decorative shaping, and teams stunningly with the Earhart Collar.

MEASUREMENTS
23cm from crown to ear
24cm wide

YARN
100g DK yarn, 1 strand

TENSION
10cm square in stocking stitch: 18 sts x 24 rows

NEEDLES AND NOTIONS
5mm knitting needles
Tapestry needle

STITCHES AND TECHNIQUES
Moss stitch
Stocking stitch
Decorative shaping

INSTRUCTIONS

Cast on 104 sts, leaving long end of yarn for sewing up. Start in moss st.
Row 1 (RS): *K1, P1, repeat from * to end.
Row 2: *P1, K1, repeat from * to end.
Repeat these two rows twice more (6 rows in total).

Decorative shaping
Row 7: K1, M1, K18, K2tog, sl1-k1-psso, K17, M1, K24, M1, K17, K2tog, sl1-k1-psso, K18, M1, K1.
Row 8: P.
Repeat these two rows 12 more times (13 times in total).

Decorative decreasing
Row 33: K1, sl1-k1-psso, K16, K2tog, sl1-k1-psso, K17, sl1-k1-psso, K20, K2tog, K17, K2tog, sl1-k1-psso, K16, K2tog, K1. 96 sts.
Row 34: P.
Row 35: K17, K2tog, sl1-k1-psso, K16, sl1-k1-psso, K18, K2tog, K16, K2tog, sl1-k1-psso, K17. 90 sts.
Row 36: P.
Row 37: K1, sl1-k1-psso, K13, K2tog, sl1-k1-psso, K15, sl1-k1-psso, K16, K2tog, K15, K2tog, sl1-k1-psso, K13, K2tog, K1. 82 sts.
Row 38: P14, PB2tog, P2tog, P14, P2tog, P14, PB2tog, P14, PB2tog, P2tog, P14. 76 sts.
Row 39: K13, K2tog, sl1-k1-psso, K13, sl1-k1-psso, K12,

K2tog, K13, K2tog, sl1-k1-psso, K13. 70 sts.

Row 40: P12, PB2tog, P2tog, P12, P2tog, P10, PB2tog, P12, PB2tog, P2tog, P12. 64 sts.

Row 41: K1, sl1-k1-psso, K8, K2tog, sl1-k1-psso, K11, sl1-k1-psso, K8, K2tog, K11, K2tog, sl1-k1-psso, K8, K2tog, K1. 56 sts.

Row 42: P9, PB2tog, P2tog, P10, P2tog, P6, PB2tog, P10, PB2tog, P2tog, P9. 50 sts.

Row 43: K1, sl1-k1-psso, K5, K2tog, sl1-k1-psso, K9, sl1-k1-psso, K4, K2tog, K9, K2tog, sl1-k1-psso, K5, K2tog, K1. 42 sts.

Row 44: P6, PB2tog, P2tog, P8, P2tog, P2, PB2tog, P8, PB2tog, P2tog, P6. 36 sts.

Row 45: K5, K2tog, sl1-k1-psso, K7, sl1-k1-psso, K2tog, K7, K2tog, sl1-k1-psso, K5. 30 sts.

Row 46: P4, PB2tog, P2tog, P6, P2tog, P6, PB2tog, P2tog, P4. 25 sts.

Row 47: K3, K2tog, sl1-k1-psso, K4, sl2tog-k1-psso, K4, K2tog, sl1-k1-psso, K3. 19 sts.

Row 48: P2, PB2tog, P2tog, P7, PB2tog, P2tog, P2. 15 sts.

Row 49: K1, K2tog, sl1-k1-psso, K5, K2tog, sl1-k1-psso, K1. 11 sts.

Row 50: PB2tog, P2tog, P3, PB2tog, P2tog. 7 sts.

TO MAKE UP

Cut off the yarn, leaving a long end. Using the tapestry needle, thread the yarn through the remaining stitches and pull tightly, avoiding puckering. Sew in the end, securing the stitches.

Sew up the edges from brim to crown. Sew in the loose ends.

DOUBLE-BREASTED COLLAR SCARF

Liverpool Street station, rush hour. . . City boys in their suits, jackets and ties, flooding out from commuter trains into the pouring London rain, inspired this scarf. It's designed to mimic the line of the collared suit for the steely professional to keep up appearances. It's smart and functional with an edge of superiority over cold, windswept peers.

MEASUREMENTS

Herringbone panel: 50cm long x 25cm wide

Moss stitch panel: 50cm long x 25cm wide

Accidental rib panel (x 2): 80cm long x 20cm wide

YARN

600g Aran yarn, 1 strand

TENSION

10cm square in herringbone pattern: 13 sts x 20 rows

10cm square in moss stitch: 13 sts x 22 rows

NEEDLES AND NOTIONS

5mm knitting needles

Tapestry needle

STITCHES AND TECHNIQUES

Herringbone pattern

Accidental rib

Moss stitch

SPECIAL ABBREVIATIONS

K1B Back From the top, insert the point of the right-hand needle into the back of the stitch below the next stitch on the left-hand needle and knit it

NOTES

The scarf is knitted in four panels that are sewn together later.

INSTRUCTIONS

Herringbone panel

Cast on 36 sts leaving long end of yarn for sewing up.

Row 1 (WS): P.

Row 2: *K2tog, K2, K1B Back, then knit st above, K2, repeat from * to last st, K1.

Row 3: P.

Row 4: K3, K1B Back, then knit st above, K2, K2tog, *K2, K1B Back, then knit st above, K2, K2tog, repeat from * to end.

Repeat these 4 rows for herringbone pattern until work measures 50cm. Cast off.

Moss stitch panel

Cast on 35 sts, leaving long end of yarn for sewing up.

Work in moss st as follows:

Row 1: *K1, P1, repeat from * to last st, K1.

Continue in moss st until work measures 50cm.

Cast off.

Accidental rib panel (Make 2)

Cast on 47 sts.

Row 1: *K2, P2, repeat from * to last 3 sts, K3.

Repeat this row for accidental rib until work measures 80cm. Cast off loosely in rib or using a crochet cast

off. Leave a long end of yarn for sewing onto main panel.

TO MAKE UP

Match up the herringbone and moss stitch panels, making sure the right side of the herringbone is facing out. Sew them together all around the edges to make the main collar panel.

Now sew the cast-off edge of the rib panel onto one short side of the main collar panel, but only halfway along both. Keep the rib relaxed while sewing it in place. Mirror for the other rib panel. Sew in loose ends.

DIAMOND GLOVES

GLOVE (*noun*) a covering for the hand worn as protection against the cold, the rough and the dirty. When fishermen braved the icy oceans kitted out in traditional hand knits, their women knitted symbolic protections into the patterning. Diamond knit represented prosperity. Here we can all have prosperity in our own hands. With a reversed stocking stitch palm, and wrist and fingers banded with functional ribs, these will fit like a glove.

MEASUREMENTS
26cm long x 9cm wide

YARN
100g Aran yarn, 1 strand

TENSION
10cm square in reversed stocking stitch: 14 sts x 19 rows

NEEDLES AND NOTIONS
6mm knitting needles
Cable needle
Tapestry needle

STITCHES AND TECHNIQUES
2 x 2 rib
Reversed stocking stitch
Cabling
Moss stitch

NOTES
(P) and (K) denotes P or K while twisting 3 back (T3B) or front (T3F)
<> Denotes centre of the diamond

INSTRUCTIONS

LEFT GLOVE
Cast on 29 sts, leaving long end of yarn for sewing up.
Row 1: *K2, P2, repeat from * to last st, K1.
Row 2: P1, *K2, P2, repeat from * to end.
Repeat these 2 rows 4 more times. 10 rows completed.

Diamond pattern
Row 1 (RS): P9, C5B, P to last st, M1, P1. 30 sts.
Row 2: K16, P5, K to end.
Row 3: P8, T3B(K), P1, T3F(K), P to end.
Row 4: K15, P2, K1, P1, K1, P2, K to end.
Row 5: P7, T3B(P), K1, P1, K1, T3F(P), P to end.
Row 6: K14, P2, [P1, K1] twice, P3, K to end.
Row 7: P6, T3B(K), [P1, K1] twice, P1, T3F(K), P to end.
Row 8: K13, P2, [K1, P1] 3 times, K1, P2, K to end.
Row 9: P5, T3B(P), [K1, P1] 3 times, K1, T3F(P), P to end.
Row 10: <> K12, P2, [P1, K1] 4 times, P3, K to end.
Row 11: P5, T3F(P), [K1, P1] 3 times, K1, T3B(P), P to end.
Row 12: K13, P2, [K1, P1] 3 times, K1, P2, K to end.
Row 13: P6, T3F(P), [P1, K1] twice, P1, T3B(P), P to end.

Row 14: K14, P2, [P1, K1] twice, P3, K to end.

Row 15: P7, T3F(P), K1, P1, K1, T3B(P), P to end.

Row 16: K15, P2, K1, P1, K1, P2, K to end.

Row 17: P8, T3F(P), P1, T3B(P), P to end.

Row 18: K16, P5, K to end.

Repeat rows 1–18 once more, omitting 1 st increase on row 1.

Row 37: P9, C5B, P to last st, P2tog, P1. 29 sts.

Finger band rib

Row 38: *K2, P2, repeat from * to last st, K1.

Row 39: P1, *K2, P2, repeat from * to end.

Repeat last 2 rows once more.

Cast off loosely in rib or using crochet hook method, leaving long end for sewing up.

RIGHT GLOVE

Work wrist rib and diamond pattern as for left glove, remembering to work C5F instead of C5B and mirror reversed st st palm, e.g.

Row 1: P16, C5F, P to last st, M1, P1.

Finger band rib

Row 38: *P2, K2, repeat from * to last st, P1.

Row 39: K1, *P2, K2, repeat from * to end.

Repeat last 2 rows once more. Cast off leaving long end of yarn.

TO MAKE UP

Sew the side edges together, from the cast-off edge to the top of the thumb opening (about 5cm) and from the cast-on edge upwards, leaving a 5cm hole for the thumb. Sew in the loose ends.

MOSS ETERNITY SCARF

ETERNITY *(noun)* from Latin *aeternitas*, without beginning or end.

The simple bands of moss stitch create a firm texture for this eternity scarf - a sculptural knit to wrap around yourself against the cold. Moss stitch is simple for the complete beginner - you just alternate knit and purl stitches to make a great reversible stitch that holds its shape. You could work up to the full scarf by making the smaller Moss Headband on page 66, first.

'ALWAYS LEAVE A LONG ENOUGH PIECE OF WOOL WHEN CASTING ON TO SEW THE FINISHED GARMENT UP WITH - SAVES TIDYING AWAY YET ANOTHER END. DO THIS ALSO WHEN KNITTING A SCARF WITH A FRINGE - THE END BECOMES A PART OF THE FRINGE. AGAIN, ALWAYS THINK AHEAD TO MAKE THE FINISHED GARMENT AS TIDY AS POSSIBLE WHEN SEWING UP.'
SHIRLEY

MEASUREMENTS
127cm long all round x 20cm deep

YARN
220g Aran yarn, 1 strand

TENSION
10cm square in moss stitch: 13 sts x 23 rows

NEEDLES AND NOTIONS
6mm knitting needles
Tapestry needle

STITCHES AND TECHNIQUES
Moss stitch

INSTRUCTIONS

Cast on 29 sts, leaving long end of yarn for sewing up.
Work in moss st as follows:
Row 1: *K1, P1, repeat from * to last st, K1.

Repeat this row until work measures 127cm.
Cast off.

Alternative cast off method
Finish knitting the final row on the right side, then fold in half with the right sides together. Cast off by knitting through the first stitch and the corresponding stitch on the cast-on edge. Repeat with the second stitch and pass the first stitch over. Continue until all stitches have been cast off, then sew the end of yarn neatly into the cast off stitches.

TO MAKE UP
Sew the cast-on and cast-off edges together neatly. Sew the loose ends into the scarf rather than along the outer edges.

MOSS HEADBAND

Fantastic for keeping off the chill and protecting our ears without messing up our hair. This headband is simple to knit, making it a great first project. Make it beautiful by keeping the edges neat and the sewing up seamless. Knit it to fit your head and it will keep its shape thanks to the wool's natural stretch and the elasticity of moss stitch.

MEASUREMENTS
48cm long all round x 10cm deep

YARN
80g Aran yarn, 1 strand

TENSION
10cm square in moss st: 13 sts x 23 rows

NEEDLES AND NOTIONS
6mm knitting needles
Tapestry needle

STITCHES AND TECHNIQUES
Moss stitch

INSTRUCTIONS

Cast on 13 sts leaving long end of yarn for sewing up.
Work in moss st as follows:
Row 1: *K1, P1, repeat from * to last st, K1.
Repeat this row until work measures 48cm long.
Cast off.

TO MAKE UP
Sew the cast-on and cast-off edges together neatly.
Sew the loose ends into the headband rather than along the outer edges.

'THUMB CAST ON: TO WORK OUT HOW MUCH YARN TO LEAVE TO START THE CAST-ON LOOP, DIVIDE THE NUMBER OF STITCHES TO BE CAST ON BY TEN. WIND THE YARN AROUND THE NEEDLE TEN TIMES AND HOLD WHERE THIS ENDS. USE THAT LENGTH AS A GUIDE TO MEASURE OUT THE NUMBER AND MAKE YOUR FIRST LOOP AT THAT POINT.'
CAROLE CARR

DRIFT CABLE HEADBAND

This headband is a Celtic plait of dense cabling. Wear it as a crown over your ears, with your ski bunny gear or rock tees, to keep off the winter chill.

MEASUREMENTS
52cm all round x 8cm deep

YARN
85g Aran yarn, 1 strand

TENSION
10cm square in stocking stitch: 14 sts x 19 rows

NEEDLES AND NOTIONS
6mm knitting needles
Cable needle
Tapestry needle

STITCHES AND TECHNIQUES
Cabling
Grafting, optional

INSTRUCTIONS

Cast on 25 sts.
Row 1 (RS): K3, *P4, K6, repeat from * to last 2 sts, P2.
Row 2: K2, *P6, K4, repeat from * to last 3 sts, P3.
Row 3: K3, *P4, C6F, repeat from * to last 2 sts, P2.
Row 4: K2, *P6, K4, repeat from * to last 3 sts, P3.
Row 5: *T5F, T5B, repeat from * to last 5 sts, T5F.
Row 6: P3, *K4, P6, repeat from * to last 2 sts, K2.
Row 7: P2, *C6B, P4, repeat from * to last 3 sts, K3.
Row 8: As row 6.
Row 9: *T5B, T5F, repeat from * to last 5 sts, T5B.
Row 10: As row 4.
Repeat rows 3–10 eleven more times (12 repeats in total), but stopping at row 9 on final repeat.
Cast off or keep sts on needle for grafting.

TO MAKE UP
Either sew the edges together or graft the stitches on the needle to the stitches just ahead of the cast-on edge, following the cabling. Sew in the loose ends.

CROCHET BEANIE

This hat inspires the feeling of the carefree 1970s. Get your crochet hook out and create a lightweight summer hat in fair-trade cotton to cover mad beach hair or heat up chilly summer evenings.

MEASUREMENTS
28cm from bottom edge to crown
22cm wide, sewn up

YARN
100g DK cotton, 1 strand

TENSION
10cm square in treble crochet: 21 sts x 10 rows

NEEDLES AND NOTIONS
3mm crochet hook
Tapestry needle

STITCHES AND TECHNIQUES
Ridged treble crochet
Double crochet
Treble crochet

CROCHET ABBREVIATIONS
ch Chain
dc Double crochet
tr Treble crochet

INSTRUCTIONS

Make 27 + 2 ch.
Work in ridged treble crochet as follows:
Foundation row: Tr in 3rd ch from hook, tr to end, make 2ch and turn (2ch are not counted as a st).
Row 1: Tr in back of loops to end, make 2ch and turn.
Repeat row 1 to complete 45 rows. Sew up band into a ring. Fasten off thread.

Crown
Work crown as one piece into top of headband, as follows:
Foundation row: Work 91dc around top of band (2dc into each row along band edge).
Work pattern by alternating dc and tr rounds (not ridged), beginning with dc round.
Work 7 repeats of pattern, ending with tr round.
14 rounds in total.

Shape crown
Work decreases only on dc rounds (apart from last round), as follows:
Round 1: [5dc, 1dc into next 2 tr] 13 times. 78 sts.
Round 2 and all alternate rounds: tr.
Round 3: [4dc, 1dc into next 2tr] 13 times. 65 sts.
Round 5: [3dc, 1dc into next 2tr] 13 times. 52 sts.
Round 7: [2dc, 1dc into next 2tr] 13 times. 39 sts.
Round 9: [1dc, 1dc into next 2tr] 13 times. 26 sts.
Round 11: [1dc into next 2tr] 13 times. 13 sts.
Round 12: [1tr into next 2 dc] 6 times, 1tr. 7 sts.
Draw yarn through loop to fasten off.

TO MAKE UP
Thread the yarn between the tops of the stitches along the top edge and draw them together. Sew in the loose ends.

BRAID CABLE NECKLACE

Carved symbols translated into knit: we found circles, crosses, triangles, letters and numbers carved into the ancient curb stones that edge their way around London's Westbourne Park. Aligned with front doors, homes of people long forgotten, the symbols hold silent stories. Enchanted by these markings, we worked triangles into the dense cabling to create this necklace scarf. Wrap it around twice or wear it as a long loop.

'DARN IT - A STITCH IN TIME SAVES NINE.'
GRAN BERYL, KETTERING

MEASUREMENTS
122cm all round x 24cm deep

YARN
400g DK yarn, 1 strand

TENSION
10cm square in stocking stitch: 20 sts x 24 rows

NEEDLES AND NOTIONS
4mm knitting needles
Cable needle
Tapestry needle

STITCHES AND TECHNIQUES
Stocking stitch
Cabling

INSTRUCTIONS

Cast on 42 sts, leaving long end of yarn for sewing up.

Triangle pattern
Row 1 (RS): P.
Row 2: K.
Row 3: K1, P9, K22, P9, K1.
Row 4 and all alternate rows: K knit sts and P purl sts.
Row 5: K1, P10, K20, P10, K1.
Row 7: K1, P11, K18, P11, K1.
Row 9: K1, P12, K16, P12, K1.
Continue in this manner until 24 rows are completed.

Row 25: P.
Row 26: K, inc 14 sts evenly along row for cable pattern.

Braid cable pattern
Row 1: K1, P3, K48, P3, K1.
Row 2 and all alternate rows: K knit sts and P purl sts.
Row 3: As row 1.
Row 5: K1, P3, [C8B] 6 times, P3, K1.
Rows 7 and 9: As row 1.
Row 11: K1, P3, K4, [C8F] 5 times, K4, P3, K1.

Row 12: As row 2.

Repeat these 12 rows for the pattern. Continue until work measures 61cm from start. Work row 2 of cable pattern once more, dec 14 sts evenly along the row. Repeat all above instructions once more. Cast off.

TO MAKE UP
Sew the cast-on and cast-off edges together neatly. Sew the loose ends into the scarf rather than along the outer edges.

CABLE HOODED SCARF

This scarf with dramatic cable patterns has a cosy hood attached to the top for really blustery days.

MEASUREMENTS
203cm long x 20cm wide

YARN
500g Aran yarn, 1 strand

TENSION
10cm square in stocking stitch: 14 sts x 19 rows

NEEDLES AND NOTIONS
6mm knitting needles
Cable needle
Tapestry needle
Stitch holder

STITCHES AND TECHNIQUES
Stocking stitch
Garter stitch
Cabling
Grafting, optional

NOTES
The cable pattern is shown between ( ).

INSTRUCTIONS

SCARF
Cast on 44 sts.
Row 1 (RS): K2, P8, (K2, P2, [K4, P2] 3 times, K2), P8, K2.
Row 2: K2, P8 (P2, [K2, P4] 3 times, K2, P2) P8, K2.
Repeat rows 1 and 2 twice more.
Row 7: K2, P8, (C12B, C12F), P8, K2.
Row 8: As row 2.
Rows 9–22: As rows 1 and 2.
Repeat rows 7–22 twenty-seven more times. 28 pattern repeats completed.
Repeat rows 7 and 8 once more, then repeat rows 1 and 2 twice more. Cast off. Measure scarf's length and mark middle point along top edge.

HOOD
Cast on 72 sts.
Row 1 (RS): K2, P2, K6, P2, K48, P2, K6, P2, K2.
Row 2: K knit sts and P purl sts.
Row 3: K2, P2, C6B, P2, K48, P2, C6B, P2, K2.
Row 4: As row 2.
Rows 5–12: As rows 1 and 2.
Repeat these 12 rows twice more. 36 rows completed.

Shape hood
Row 37: K2, P2, K6, P2, K21, K2tog, K1. 35 sts.
Slip remaining 36 sts for left side of hood onto holding needle.

Continuing cable pattern, dec 1 st at left edge only (K2tog, K1 on RS; P1, P2tog on WS) on rows 40, 43, 45, 47, 49, 51, 53, 55, 56. 26 sts.

Cast off or slip sts onto holding needle for grafting. Mirror shaping for left side of hood as follows: Work 36 sts from holding needle. Dec 1 st at right edge only (K1, K2tog on RS; P2tog, P1 on WS) on rows 37, 40, 43, 45, 47, 49, 51, 53, 55, 56. Cast off or keep sts on needle for grafting.

TO MAKE UP

Sew or graft the stitches from both top sides of the hood together. Sew the curved edges together. Seam hood to middle of scarf, ensuring you match the marked middle point with the centre of the back of the hood. Sew in the loose ends.

HOUNDSTOOTH GLOVES

Make these functional fingerless gloves with a striking houndstooth pattern to match the Houndstooth Bobble Hat on page 82.

Houndstooth is a traditional Scottish pattern for woven wool, translated here into these bold knitted gloves. You can use vivid colour play to create striking contrasts in the tessilated patterning. We love jet black and red, but also try yellow and black, or blue with red.

MEASUREMENTS
19cm long x 18cm wide unsewn

YARN
100g Aran yarn, 1 strand in black (MC) and red (CC)

TENSION
10cm square in stocking stitch: 15 sts x 19 rows

NEEDLES AND NOTIONS
5mm knitting needles
Tapestry needle

STITCHES AND TECHNIQUES
1 x 1 twisted rib
Houndstooth Fair Isle pattern
Stocking stitch

NOTES
For the houndstooth pattern, make sure the main colour floats are always on top of the contrast colour floats when changing colours. This creates straight, horizontal lines at the back of the work and stops the yarn twisting.

When changing colour on the first and last stitch of each row, ensure the yarn is tight and doesn't cause loops or floats, as this will create small holes in the glove. Wrap the yarns around each other to ensure a tight yarn change.

INSTRUCTIONS

LEFT GLOVE
Using MC, cast on 34 sts, leaving long end of yarn for sewing up.

1 x 1 twisted rib
Row 1 (RS): K1, *KB1, P1, repeat from * to last st, K1.
Row 2: P1, *K1, PB1, repeat from * to last st, P1.
Repeat these two rows until 12 rows are completed. Join CC.

Pattern
Row 1 (RS): K3 in MC, [K1 in CC, K3 in MC] 4 times, K15 in MC.
Row 2: P16 in MC, [P3 in CC, P1 in MC] 4 times, P2 in MC.
Row 3: K2 in MC, [K3 in CC, K1 in MC] 4 times, K16 in MC.
Row 4: P17 in MC, [P1 in CC, P3 in MC] 4 times, P1 in MC.
Repeat rows 1–4 five more times (6 repeats in total). 24 rows of pattern completed. Break off CC.
Working across all 34 sts, in MC, complete four rows of twisted rib. Cast off loosely in rib, leaving a long end of yarn for sewing up.

RIGHT GLOVE

Start with 12 rows of twisted rib as for left glove.

Work pattern as for left glove, but with houndstooth panel positioned on opposite side of work as follows:

Row 1 (RS): K17 in MC, [K1 in CC, K3 in MC] 4 times, K1 in MC.

Row 2: P2 in MC, [P3 in CC, P1 in MC] 4 times, P16 in MC.

Row 3: K16 in MC, [K3 in CC, K1 in MC] 4 times, K2 in MC.

Row 4: P3 in MC, [P1 in CC, P3 in MC] 4 times, P15 in MC.

Repeat rows 1–4 five more times.

The rest of glove is knitted and finished as for left glove.

TO MAKE UP

Sew the side edges together from the cast-off edge to the thumb opening (about 4cm). Stitch from the cast-on edge upwards, leaving a 4cm hole for the thumb. Sew in the loose ends.

HOUNDSTOOTH BOBBLE HAT

Putting a twist on classics is at the core of our design ethos.
Looking for newness in the simple bobble hat we sought to bring heritage patterns to the top, inventing the 'knitted bobble'. Instead of wrapping yarn around a template, the bobble was knitted, gathered into a small ball and sewn to the top of the hat.

MEASUREMENTS

30cm from bottom edge to crown

23cm wide, sewn up

YARN

180g Aran yarn, 1 strand, in black (MC) and red (CC)

TENSION

10cm square in stocking stitch: 15 sts x 19 rows

NEEDLES AND NOTIONS

Small quantity of roving yarn for stuffing bobble

5mm knitting needles

Tapestry needle

STITCHES AND TECHNIQUES

1 x 1 twisted rib

Stocking stitch

Houndstooth Fair Isle pattern

NOTES

The bobble is knitted as a flat panel in the houndstooth pattern, then gathered into a ball before securing it to the hat.

For the houndstooth pattern, make sure the main colour floats are always on top of the contrast colour floats when changing colours. This creates straight, horizontal lines at the back of the work and stops the yarn twisting.

INSTRUCTIONS

HAT

Cast on 74 sts, leaving long end of yarn for sewing up.

1 x 1 twisted rib

Row 1 (RS): P1, *KB1, P1, repeat from * to last st, P1.

Row 2: K1, *K1, PB1, repeat from * to last st, K1.

Work 1 x 1 twisted rib for 29 rows in total. Rib section measures about 15cm.

Crown

Start with WS facing, as twisted rib will be folded later to show on RS.

Row 30 (WS becomes RS): K.

Row 31: P.

Repeat these 2 rows 7 more times. 45 rows completed.

Shape crown

Row 46: K1, *K6, K2tog, repeat from * to last st, K1.

Row 47 and all alternate rows: P.

Row 48: K1, *K5, K2tog, repeat from * to last st, K1.

Row 50: K1, *K4, K2tog, repeat from * to last st, K1.

Row 52: K1, *K3, K2tog, repeat from * to last st, K1.

Row 54: K1, *K2, K2tog, repeat from * to last st, K1.

Row 56: K1, *K1, K2tog, repeat from * to last st, K1.

Row 58: K1, *K2tog, repeat from * to last st, K1. 11 sts.

Row 59: *P2tog, repeat from * to last st, P1. 6 sts.

BOBBLE PANEL

Using MC, cast on 14 sts. Work all increases (M1) and decreases (K/P2tog) in MC.

Row 1 (RS): K.

Inc as follows:

Row 2: P1, M1, *P, repeat from * to last st, M1, P1.

Join CC.

Row 3: K1 in MC, M1, [K1 in CC, K3 in MC] 3 times,

K1 in CC, K1 in MC, M1, K1 in MC. (Four pattern repeats in a row.)

Row 4: P1 in MC, M1, [P3 in CC, P1 in MC] 4 times, M1, P1 in MC.

Row 5: K1 in MC, M1, K1 in MC, [K3 in CC, K1 in MC] 4 times, K1 in MC, M1, K1 in MC.

Row 6: P1 in MC, M1, P3 in MC, [P1 in CC, P3 in MC] 4 times, P1 in MC, M1, P1 in MC. 24 sts.

Row 7: K1 in MC, [K1 in CC, K3 in MC] 5 times, K1 in CC, K2 in MC. (Six pattern repeats in a row.)

Row 8: [P3 in CC, P1 in MC] 6 times.

Row 9: [K3 in CC, K1 in MC] 6 times.

Row 10: P1 in MC, [P1 in CC, P3 in MC] 5 times, P1 in CC, P2 in MC.

Repeat rows 7-10 twice more.

Row 19: K5 in MC, [K1 in CC, K3 in MC] 4 times, K3 in MC. (Four pattern repeats in a row.)

Dec as follows:

Row 20: P2tog, P2 in MC, [P3 in CC, P1 in MC] 4 times, P2 in MC, P2tog.

Row 21: K2tog, K1 in MC, [K3 in CC, K1 in MC] 4 times, K1 in MC, K2tog.

Row 22: P2tog, P1 in MC, [P1 in CC, P3 in MC] 3 times, P1 in CC, P2 in MC, P2tog. Break off CC. Continue in MC.

Row 23: K2tog, K to last 2 sts, K2tog.

Row 24: P2tog, P to last 2 sts, P2tog.

Cast off remaining 14 sts, leaving long end.

TO MAKE UP

Using the tapestry needle, thread the yarn through the remaining stitches of the hat and pull tightly, avoiding puckering. Sew in the end, securing the stitches.

Starting on the wrong side (for the rib will be turned wrong side out later), sew the rib edges together for two-thirds of the way up (about 9cm) from the cast-on edge. Turn to the right side and continue stitching to the top of the crown.

Stuff the bobble panel with roving yarn. Draw the edges in with a thread, securing the content. Make a bobble, by tying the centre tightly, and fasten it on top of the hat. Sew in the loose ends.

LADDER NECKLACE

This lacy eternity scarf is formed by rows of ladder (drop) stitch, which ascend and descend round and round. The alternate wrapping and releasing of stitches makes a light web, as with a string vest, trapping the air closely to us in pockets of warmth.

MEASUREMENTS
164cm all round x 28cm deep

YARN
200g DK yarn, 1 strand

TENSION
Due to the open nature of ladder st, the tension is not particularly important; instead just make sure your scarf is the right length.

NEEDLES AND NOTIONS
5mm knitting needles
Tapestry needle

STITCHES AND TECHNIQUES
Ladder (drop) stitch
Garter stitch

SPECIAL ABBREVIATIONS
K and D Knit first wrap, then drop other wraps per stitch

Wrap 2 Ladder stitch, wrapping yarn twice around needle, repeated to end of row

Wrap 4 Ladder stitch, wrapping yarn 4 times around needle, repeated to end of row

Wrap 6 Ladder stitch, wrapping yarn 6 times around needle, repeated to end of row

LADDER (DROP) STITCH
Insert the right-hand needle knitwise into the first stitch and wrap the yarn around the specified number of times. Pull the wrapped yarn through the stitch as in ordinary knitting. Work in this manner to the end of row.

On the next row, knit all the stitches normally, releasing (dropping) the wrapped stitches as you go.

INSTRUCTIONS

Cast on 49 sts, leaving long end of yarn for sewing up.
K 4 rows. Next row Wrap 4. Next row K and D.
K 3 rows. Next row Wrap 2. Next row K and D.
K 1 row. Next row Wrap 2. Next row K and D.
K 3 rows. Next row Wrap 6. Next row K and D.
K 9 rows. Next row Wrap 2. Next row K and D.
K 1 row. Next row Wrap 2. Next row K and D.
K 3 rows. Next row Wrap 4. Next row K and D.
Repeat last 5 rows once more.
K 1 row. Next row Wrap 2. Next row K and D.
Repeat last 3 rows once more.
K 5 rows. Next row Wrap 6. Next row K and D.
K 3 rows. Next row Wrap 4. Next row K and D.
K 3 rows. Next row Wrap 2. Next row K and D.
K 5 rows. Next row Wrap 2. Next row K and D.
K 1 row. Next row Wrap 4. Next row K and D.
K 1 row. Next row Wrap 2. Next row K and D.
K 3 rows. Next row Wrap 2. Next row K and D.
K 7 rows. Next row Wrap 6. Next row K and D.
K 3 rows. Next row Wrap 4. Next row K and D.
K 1 row. Next row Wrap 2. Next row K and D.
K 3 rows. Next row Wrap 2. Next row K and D.

K 1 row. Next row Wrap 4. Next row K and D.
K 3 rows. Next row Wrap 6. Next row K and D.
K 7 rows. Next row Wrap 2. Next row K and D.
K 3 rows. Next row Wrap 2. Next row K and D.
K 1 rows. Next row Wrap 2. Next row K and D.
K 3 rows. Next row Wrap 2. Next row K and D.
K 1 row. Next Wrap 4. Next row K and D.
K 1 row. Next row Wrap 2. Next row K and D.
K 4 rows. Next row Wrap 2. Next row K and D.
K 3 rows. Next row Wrap 4. Next row K and D.
K 3 rows. Next row Wrap 6. Next row K and D.
K 5 rows. Next row Wrap 2. Next row K and D.
K 1 row. Next row Wrap 2. Next row K and D.
Repeat last 3 rows.

K 1 row. Next row Wrap 4. Next row K and D.
K 3 rows. Next row Wrap 4. Next row K and D.
K 3 rows. Next row Wrap 2. Next row K and D.
K 1 row. Next row Wrap 2. Next row K and D.
K 9 rows. Next row Wrap 6. Next row K and D.
K 3 rows. Next row Wrap 2. Next row K and D.
K 1 row. Next row Wrap 2. Next row K and D.
K 3 rows. Next row Wrap 4. Next row K and D.
K 1 row. Cast off.

TO MAKE UP
Sew the cast-on and cast-off edges together neatly.
Sew in the loose ends.

'The North Circular's thoughtfully made knits are luxurious timeless pieces that you will treasure for a lifetime.' *AMBER VALLETTA*

URCHIN BERET

Henry, aged 96, the most stylish man I ever met, always greeted you with 'How are you, darling?' He left me some beautiful giant sea urchins, which, when you hold them up to the light, reveal pinprick lines of holes running in rivers around the shell. We decided they looked like a fantastic headpiece and set about translating them into this beret. The linen stitch gradually becomes smaller and smaller as it moves down from the crown, until it forms tiny tight stitches around the bottom band.

MEASUREMENTS
21cm from bottom edge to crown

YARN
100g DK yarn, 1 strand

TENSION
10cm square in linen stitch: 16 sts x 22 rows
Linen stitch requires very even tension.

NEEDLES AND NOTIONS
5mm DPNs *
6mm DPNs *
8mm DPNs *
10mm DPNs *
Stitch markers
Tapestry needle

* This hat can be knitted entirely on double-pointed needles and, for ease, two sets of 10mm DPNs are recommended.

STITCHES AND TECHNIQUES
Linen stitch
Circular knitting

NOTES
Rather than increasing stitches, this hat gets wider by using bigger needles.

Conventionally, linen stitch makes a very dense, inflexible, woven-looking fabric. But by using much bigger needles, an open honeycomb lace effect is created.

All slipped stitches are slipped purlwise. Be careful as it is easy to purl the occasional stitch instead of slipping it when you put yarn forward.

Keep sts between DPNs tight to avoid gaps.

INSTRUCTIONS

Using 5mm DPNs, cast on 91 sts. Join, being careful not to twist sts, PM at beginning of round.

Linen stitch pattern
Round 1: *K1, sl1 wyf, repeat from * to last st, K1.
Round 2: *Sl1 wyf, K1, repeat from * to last st, sl1 wyf.
Repeat these 2 rounds, changing needle size as follows:
Rounds 1–10: 5mm (10 rounds).
Rounds 11–14: 6mm (4 rounds).
Rounds 15–18: 8mm (4 rounds).
Rounds 19–36: 10mm (18 rounds).

Shape crown
Continue on 10mm DPNs.
Round 37: [K1, sl1 wyf] 4 times, [sl2tog-k1-psso, (sl1 wyf, K1) 7 times, sl1 wyf] 4 times, sl2tog-k1-psso, [sl1 wyf, K1] 4 times.
Round 38: As round 2.
Round 39: As round 1.
Round 40: [Sl1 wyf, K1] 3 times, sl1 wyf, [sl2tog-k1-psso, (sl1 wyf, K1) 6 times, sl1 wyf] 4 times, sl2tog-k1-psso, [sl1 wyf, K1] 3 times, sl1 wyf.
Round 41: As round 1.
Round 42: As round 2.
Round 43: [K1, sl1 wyf] 3 times, [sl2tog-k1-psso, (sl1 wyf, K1) 5 times, sl1 wyf] 4 times, sl2tog-k1-psso, [sl1 wyf, K1] 3 times.
Round 44: As round 2.
Round 45: As round 1.
Round 46: [Sl1 wyf, K1] twice, sl1 wyf, [sl2tog-k1-psso, (sl1 wyf, K1) 4 times, sl1 wyf] 4 times, sl2tog-k1-psso, [sl1 wyf, K1] twice, sl1 wyf.
Round 47: As round 1.
Round 48: As round 2.

Round 49: [K1, sl1 wyf] twice, [sl2tog-k1-psso, (sl1 wyf, K1) 3 times, sl1 wyf] 4 times, sl2tog-k1-psso, [sl1 wyf, K1] twice.

Round 50: As round 2.

Round 51: As round 1.

Round 52: Sl1 wyf, K1, sl1 wyf, [sl2tog-k1-psso, (sl1 wyf, K1) twice, sl1 wyf] 4 times, sl2tog-k1-psso, sl1 wyf, K1, sl1 wyf.

Round 53: As round 1.

Round 54: As round 2.

Round 55: K1, sl1 wyf, [sl2tog-k1-psso, sl1 wyf, K1, sl1 wyf] 4 times, sl2tog-k1-psso, sl1 wyf, K1.

Change to 5mm DPNs.

Round 56: Sl1 wyf, [sl2tog-k1-psso, (sl1 wyf, K1)] 5 times.

Round 57: K1, [K2tog] 5 times.

TO MAKE UP

Draw the yarn through the remaining stitches. Sew in the loose ends.

'Using needles that are a bit small for the yarn will end up with a very tight knit, which will `felt' when washed. Practice ensures the feel of the wool and needles together feels right.'
SHIRLEY HUNT

CATCH SHRUG

TO SHRUG *(verb)* to raise and lower the shoulders in order to convey disinterest, nonchalance, glamour, aloofness.

In London's day-to-night city, every girl perfects the up-down look. Don't try too hard – maybe a vintage 1920s crushed velvet dress that once danced on the steamliners to New York, worn with pirate boots and chunky cuffs. Do away with the fur stole and throw over this 20s-inspired shrug, cables enhancing your shoulders and wrapping you up – smoking hot! The knitted holes add movement to this shrug, so it can be gathered around the neck or pulled firmly down over the shoulders.

MEASUREMENTS
38cm wide at top, sewn up
50cm wide at bottom, sewn up
48cm deep

YARN
560g Aran yarn, 1 strand

TENSION
10cm square in stocking stitch: 14 sts x 19 rows

NEEDLES AND NOTIONS
6mm knitting needles
Cable needle
Tapestry needle

STITCHES AND TECHNIQUES
Cabling
Garter stitch
Lace knitting

NOTES
The shrug is knitted in three panels that are sewn together later.
The cable pattern is shown between ( ).

INSTRUCTIONS

Bottom panel
Cast on 42 sts, leaving long end of yarn for sewing up.
Row 1: K2, [yo, sl1-k1-psso] twice, P2, C4B, K2, P2, (K2, [P2, K4] 3 times, P2, K2), P2.
Row 2 and all alternate rows: K knit sts and P purl sts.
Row 3: K2, [yo, sl1-k1-psso] twice, P2, K2, C4F, P2 (K2, [P2, K4] 3 times, P2, K2), P2.
Row 5: As row 1.
Row 7: K2, [yo, sl1-k1-psso] twice, P2, K2, C4F, P2 (C12B, C12F), P2.
Row 9: As row 1.
Row 11: As row 3.
Row 13: As row 1.
Row 15: As row 3.
Row 17: As row 1.
Row 19: As row 3.
Row 21: As row 1.
Row 22: As row 2.
Repeat rows 7–22 until work measures about 96cm.
Work rows 7–9 once more. Cast off.

Middle panel

Cast on 23 sts, leaving long end of yarn for sewing up.

Row 1: P8, K1, [yo, sl1-k1-psso] 3 times, P8.

Row 2: P.

Repeat these two rows until work measures about 86cm. Cast off.

Top panel

Cast on 36 sts, leaving long end of yarn for sewing up.

Row 1: P2, (K2, [P2, K4] 3 times, P2, K2), P2, C4B, K2, P2.

Row 2 and all alternate rows: K knit sts and P purl sts.

Row 3: P2, (K2, [P2, K4] 3 times, P2, K2), P2, K2, C4F, P2.

Row 5: As row 1.

Row 7: P2, (C12B, C12F), P2, K2, C4F, P2.

Row 9: As row 1.

Row 11: As row 3.

Row 13: As row 1.

Row 15: As row 3.

Row 17: As row 1.

Row 19: As row 3.

Row 21: As row 1.

Row 22: As row 2.

Repeat rows 7–22 until work measures about 76cm. Work rows 7–9 once more. Cast off.

TO MAKE UP

Sew the panels together side by side, making sure the cable plaits are on the outsides of the panels (at the top and bottom). You will need to ease the bottom panel into the middle one and the middle panel into the top one. Then sew the two ends together to make a tube. Sew in the loose ends.

AERO HAT

This is the ultimate jaunty hat. Sporting it, snowboarders will fly off the slopes with an extra flourish as the tassel takes off!

   This hat is not meant to be taken seriously – adorned with a large cable, it's a light-hearted affair that can be worn at any angle to please the wearer. Team it with the Hunter Scarf on page 106.

MEASUREMENTS
34cm from bottom edge to crown
22cm wide, sewn up
15.5cm long tassel

YARN
150g DK yarn, 1 strand

TENSION
10cm square in stocking stitch: 20 sts x 24 rows

NEEDLES AND NOTIONS
4mm knitting needles
Cable needle
Tapestry needle
Card to make tassel template
3.5mm knitting needles, optional for firmer rib

STITCHES AND TECHNIQUES
2 x 2 rib
Cabling
Tassel

INSTRUCTIONS

Cast on 90 sts, leaving long end of yarn for sewing up.

2 x 2 rib
Row 1: *P2, K2, repeat from * to last 2 sts, P2.
Row 2: K2, *P2, K2, repeat from * to end.
Repeat these 2 rows until 34 rows are completed.

Crown with cable pattern
Row 1: K32, P2, K6, [P2, K2] twice, P2, K6, P2, K32.
Row 2 and all alternate rows: K knit sts and P purl sts.
Row 3: As row 1.
Row 5: K32, P2, C6B, [P2, K2] twice, P2, C6F, P2, K32.
Row 6: As row 2.
Repeat rows 1–6 twice more.
Row 19: As row 1.
Row 21: K32, P2, K2, [P2, K6] twice, P2, K2, P2, K32.

'... IT'S EVERYTHING A GREAT BRITISH BRAND SHOULD BE; FASHIONABLE, COOL, BRAVE BUT IT'S ALSO KIND AND ALTRUISTIC. I LOVE WHAT IT STANDS FOR AND LOVE WEARING IT.'
DEEP KAILEY, FASHION DIRECTOR, TATLER MAGAZINE

Row 23: K32, P2, K2, P2, C6F, P2, C6B, P2, K2, P2, K32.

Row 25: As row 21.

Row 26: As row 2.

Repeat rows 21–26 twice more. 38 rows completed.

Shape crown

Row 39: K30, sl1-k1-psso, P2, K6, [P2, K2] twice, P2, K6, P2, K2tog, K30. 88 sts.

Row 40 and all alternate rows up to and including row 52: K knit sts and P purl sts.

Row 41: K9, K2tog, sl1-k1-psso, K16, sl1-k1-psso, P2, C6B, [P2, K2] twice, P2, C6F, P2, K2tog, K16, K2tog, sl1-k1-psso, K9. 82 sts.

Row 43: K8, K2tog, sl1-k1-psso, K14, sl1-k1-psso, P2, K6, [P2, K2] twice, P2, K6, P2, K2tog, K14, K2tog, sl1-k1-psso, K8. 76 sts.

Row 45: K7, K2tog, sl1-k1-psso, K12, sl1-k1-psso, P2, K6, [P2, K2] twice, P2, K6, P2, K2tog, K12, K2tog, sl1-k1-psso, K7. 70 sts.

Row 47: K6, K2tog, sl1-k1-psso, K10, sl1-k1-psso, P2, C6B, [P2, K2] twice, P2, C6F, P2, K2tog, K10, K2tog, sl1-k1-psso, K6. 64 sts.

Row 49: K5, K2tog, sl1-k1-psso, K8, sl1-k1-psso, P2, K6, [P2, K2] twice, P2, K6, P2, K2tog, K8, K2tog, sl1-k1-psso, K5. 58 sts.

Row 51: K4, K2tog, sl1-k1-psso, K6, sl1-k1-psso, P2, K6, [P2, K2] twice, P2, K6, P2, K2tog, K6, K2tog, sl1-k1-psso, K4. 52 sts.

Row 53: K3, K2tog, sl1-k1-psso, K4, sl1-k1-psso, P2tog, sl3 sts onto CN, leave at back of work, K3, K3tog from CN, [P2tog, K2] twice, P2tog, sl3 sts onto CN at front of work, K3tog, K3 from CN, P2tog, K2tog, K4, K2tog, sl1-k1-psso, K3. 37 sts.

Row 54: P2, PB2tog, P2tog, P2, P2tog, K1, P2tog twice, [K1, P2] twice, K1, PB2tog twice, K1, PB2tog, P2, PB2tog, P2tog, P2. 27 sts.

Row 55: K1, K2tog, sl1-k1-psso 5 times, P1, [K2tog] 5 times, sl1-k1-psso, K1. 15 sts.

Row 56: [P2tog] 7 times, P1. 8 sts.

TO MAKE UP

Cut the yarn leaving a long end. Using the tapestry needle, thread through the remaining stitches and pull tightly, avoiding puckering. Sew in the end, securing the stitches.

Starting on the wrong side (for the rib will be turned wrong side out later), sew the edges together, to about 9cm up from cast-on edge. Turn to the right side and continue stitching to the top of the crown.

To make the tassel, cut a rectangular piece of card, 15cm wide, to use as a template. Wind the yarn round the card to the required thickness (about 40 wraps). Break the yarn, leaving a long end. Thread the yarn end through the tapestry needle. Slip the needle through all the loops at one end and tie the yarn tightly. Remove the card and wind the yarn round the loops below the fold. Make a stitch to fasten them and draw the needle through the top ready for sewing the tassel to the hat. Cut through the other fold and trim the edges. Secure the tassel to the top of the hat.

MORI COLLAR

We named this sturdy neckwarmer after the sweetest Cornish photographer – Moriarty. The giant stitches contrast with the mind-bending twists of the Celtic cables. Zip it under an oversized raincoat to brave the fiercest winter beach walks.

MEASUREMENTS
31cm wide, sewn up
27cm deep at back

YARN
550g Aran yarn, 2 strands together for moss collar, 1 strand for cable band

TENSION
10cm square in moss stitch, using 2 strands and 9mm needles: 9 sts x 16 rows

NEEDLES AND NOTIONS
6mm knitting needles
9mm knitting needles
Cable needle
Tapestry needle

STITCHES AND TECHNIQUES
Moss stitch
Cabling
Slip stitch

INSTRUCTIONS

Moss collar
Using 9mm needles and 2 strands of yarn, cast on 45 sts, leaving long end of yarn for sewing up.
Work moss st as follows:
Row 1: *K1, P1, repeat from * to last st, K1.

Repeat this row 22 times in total.

Shape collar
Dec 1 st (work 1 st, K2tog/P2tog, depending on moss st; K2tog/P2tog, work last st) on each edge of rows 23, 26, 29, 31, 33, 35, 37, 38, 39, 40, 41. 23 sts.
Inc 1 st (work 1 st, M1; M1, work last st) on each edge of rows 43, 44, 45, 46, 47, 49, 51, 53, 55, 58, 61. 45 sts.
Work 22 more rows in moss st, without shaping. Cast off.

Cable band
Cast on 25 sts, using 6mm needles and 1 strand of yarn.

Row 1 (RS): K3, *P4, K6, repeat from * to last 2 sts, P2.
Row 2: K2, *P6, K4, repeat from * to last 3 sts, P3.
Row 3: K3, *P4, C6F, repeat from* to last 2 sts, P2.
Row 4: K2, *P6, K4, repeat from* to last 3 sts, P3.
Row 5: *T5F, T5B, repeat from * to last 5 sts, T5F.
Row 6: P3, *K4, P6, repeat from * to last 2 sts, K2.
Row 7: P2, *C6B, P4, repeat from * to last 3 sts, K3.
Row 8: As row 6.
Row 9: *T5B, T5F, repeat from * to last 5 sts, T5B.
Row 10: As row 4.
Repeat rows 3–10 twenty-four more times (25 repeats in total). Cast off.

TO MAKE UP

Mark 10cm up from the cast-on and cast-off edges. Starting at the cast-on edges, place the cable band right sides and both points A together with the main collar. Sew them together along the shaped edge to 10cm from the cast-off edge of the main collar.

With right sides and edges C together, and starting at the cast-on edge again, sew the edges together for 10cm. Then sew edges D together, starting at the cast-off edge, to meet the sewn edge of C. Then sew the two B edges together, matching the fold in the cable band to the 10cm marker on edge C as a starting point.

When the cable band has been attached to the main collar, turn inside out and sew the edges of the cable band together as appropriate. Turn right side out and slip stitch the cast-on edge to the cast-off edge of the main collar and cable band to produce an almost invisible join.

HUNTER SCARF

SCARF *(noun)* a length of knitted fabric worn around the neck.

This particular scarf is named after one of our amazing knitters, whose name evokes brave hunters treading the snowy paths of old. It's an everyday classic in thick Aran yarn, with cables twisting down, flanked by sturdy thick ribbing.

MEASUREMENTS
173cm long x 18cm wide

YARN
475g Aran yarn, 1 strand

TENSION
10cm square in accidental rib, measured relaxed:
22 sts x 22 rows

NEEDLES AND NOTIONS
6mm knitting needles
Cable needle
Tapestry needle

STITCHES AND TECHNIQUES
Accidental rib
Cabling

NOTES
The cable pattern is shown between ( ).

INSTRUCTIONS

Cast on 43 sts.

Accidental rib
Row 1 (RS): *K2, P2, repeat from * to last 3 sts, K3.
Repeat this row 14 times.

Cable pattern
Row 1: [K2, P2] twice, K3, (K2, P2 [K6, P2] twice, K2), K1, P2, K2, P2, K3.
Row 2: [K2, P2] twice, K2, (P2, [K2, P6] twice, K2, P2), [K2, P2] twice, K3.
Row 3: [K2, P2] twice, K3, (K2, P2, C6F, P2, C6B, P2, K2), K1, P2, K2, P2, K3.
Row 4: As row 2.
Row 5: As row 1.
Row 6: As row 2.

Rows 7–12: Repeat last 6 rows once more.

Row 13: [K2, P2] twice, K3, (K6, P2, [K2, P2] twice, K6), K1, P2, K2, P2, K3.

Row 14: [K2, P2] twice, K2, (P6, [K2, P2] twice, K2, P6), [K2, P2] twice, K3.

Row 15: [K2, P2] twice, K3, (C6B, P2, [K2, P2] twice, C6F), K1, P2, K2, P2, K3.

Row 16: As row 14.

Row 17: As row 13.

Row 18: As row 14.

Rows 19–24: Repeat last 6 rows once more.

Repeat rows 1–24 twelve more times (13 repeats in total).

Knit 14 rows of accidental rib as at beginning of scarf.

Cast off loosely in pattern or using crochet cast-off method.

TO MAKE UP

Sew in the loose ends.

KNEE SOCKS

At the onset of the First World War, Lord Kitchener called upon the women to arm themselves with needles and knit socks for their country. Credited with his own sock design, he championed a seamless grafting stitch that made the socks for the troops more comfortable to wear. It became known as the Kitchener stitch and it still makes for a classic sock design. Knit these socks for your own troops or a nice pair for yourself as this useful design suits all down to the ground. The contrasting cuff is long enough to peek over the top of boots and wellies as you brave dark and starry evening jaunts to the nearest pub.

MEASUREMENTS
37cm long from heel to cuff
9cm wide cuff
Length of foot adaptable

YARN
160g DK yarn, 1 strand, 110g in navy (MC) and 50g in black (CC)

TENSION
10cm square in stocking stitch: 20 sts x 26 rows

NEEDLES AND NOTIONS
Set of 3.75mm double-pointed knitting needles
Place markers
Stitch holder
Tapestry needle

STITCHES AND TECHNIQUES
1 x 1 rib
3 x 1 rib
Stocking stitch
Circular knitting
Grafting

INSTRUCTIONS

Using CC, cast on 52 sts. Divide sts between three DPNs (18, 16, 18). Join, being careful not to twist cast-on row sts. PM at beginning of round.

1 x 1 rib
Work in 1 x 1 rib, as follows:
Round 1: *K1, P1, repeat from * to end.
Repeat this round for pattern.
Continue in rib for 9cm. Break off CC.
Change to MC and continue in 3 x 1 rib as follows:
Round 1: *K3, P1, repeat from * to end.
Repeat this round for pattern.
Continue in rib for 9cm.

Shape leg
Continue keeping 3 x 1 rib pattern.
Round 1: K1, sl1-k1-psso, P1, rib to end of 1st needle; rib all sts on 2nd needle; rib sts on 3rd needle to last 4 sts, K2tog, K1, P1.

Rib 9 rounds without shaping but K2, not 3, at beginning of 1st needle and K2, P1 at end of 3rd needle in every round to keep rib pattern.

Round 11: K1, sl1-k1-psso, K3, rib to end of 1st needle; rib all sts on 2nd needle; rib sts on 3rd needle to last 7 sts, K3, K2tog, K1, P1.

Rib 9 rounds, beginning with K5 on 1st needle and ending with K5, P1 on 3rd needle.

Round 21: K1, sl1-k1-psso, K2, rib to end of 1st needle; rib all sts on 2nd needle; rib sts on 3rd needle to last 6 sts, K2, K2tog, K1, P1.

Rib 9 rounds beginning with K4 on 1st needle and ending with K4, P1 on 3rd needle.

Round 31: K1, sl1-k1-psso, K1, rib to end of 1st needle; rib all sts on 2nd needle; rib sts on 3rd needle to last 5 sts, K1, K2tog, K1, P1. 44 sts.

Continue in 3 x 1 rib until leg measures 28cm from the cast-on edge.

Divide for heel panel

The purl stitch that runs between leg decrease will be centre of heel. Divide sts for heel as follows: sl10 sts to left of centre purl stitch, slip purl stitch and sl11 sts to right of it (reverse for other sock) onto one needle (22 sts in total). Leave remaining sts on stitch holder for instep.

Work heel stitch

Rejoin MC if necessary. Work back and forth in rows as follows, slipping sts purlwise.

Row 1 (RS): *Sl1, K1, repeat from * to end.
Row 2: Sl1, *P, repeat from * to end.
Work 22 rows in total.

Turn heel

Row 1 (RS): K13, sl1-k1-psso, K1, turn work.
Row 2: Sl1, P5, P2tog, P1, turn work.
Row 3: Sl1, K6, sl1-k1-psso, K1, turn work.
Row 4: Sl1, P7, P2tog, P1, turn work.

Row 5: Sl1, K8, sl1-k1-psso, K1, turn work.
Row 6: Sl1, P9, P2tog, P1, turn work.
Row 7: Sl1, K10, sl1-k1-psso, K1.
Row 8: Sl1, P11, P2tog, P1.
Row 9: Sl1, K11, sl1-k1-psso.
Row 10: Sl1, P10, P2tog. 12 sts.

Shape gusset

Onto 1st needle, K all 12 heel sts, then pick up and K11 sts along adjacent side of heel panel. Onto 2nd needle, pick up and rib 22 sts from stitch holder. Onto 3rd needle, pick up and K11 sts along opposite side of heel panel, then K first 6 sts from 1st needle. Stitches are divided as follows: 17 sts on 1st needle, 22 sts on 2nd needle, 17 sts on 3rd needle. 56 sts.

Next round: K to last 3 sts on 1st needle, K2tog, K1; rib all sts on 2nd needle; K1, sl1-k1-psso, K to end of 3rd needle. 54 sts.
Next round: K to end of 1st needle; rib all sts on 2nd needle; K to end of 3rd needle.
Repeat these 2 rounds 6 times in total. (44 sts remaining: 11 sts on 1st and 3rd needles, 22 sts on 2nd needle.)

Foot

Continue as set, working sts on 1st and 3rd needles in st st and sts on 2nd needle in 3 x 1 rib, until work measures 5cm less than desired length (see chart opposite for shoe size / foot conversions). Break off MC.

Shape toe

Change to CC and continue in st st.
Round 1: K to last 3 sts on 1st needle, K2tog, K1; K1, sl1-k1-psso, K to last 3 sts on 2nd needle, K2tog, K1; K1, sl1-k1-psso, K to end of 3rd needle. 40 sts.
Round 2: K.
Repeat these 2 rounds 7 times in total. 16 sts.

K sts from 1st needle onto 3rd needle. Break off yarn, leaving 15cm end.

TO MAKE UP

Graft the toe stitches from the second needle to stitches on the third needle. Sew in the loose ends.

Women's shoe size to foot length conversions

UK	3	3½	4	4½	5	5½	6	6½	7	7½	8	8½	9
EU	35–36	36	36–37	37	37–38	38	38–39	39	39–40	40	40–41	41	41–42
Length	21.6	22.2	22.5	23	23.5	23.8	24.1	24.6	25.1	25.4	25.9	26.2	26.7

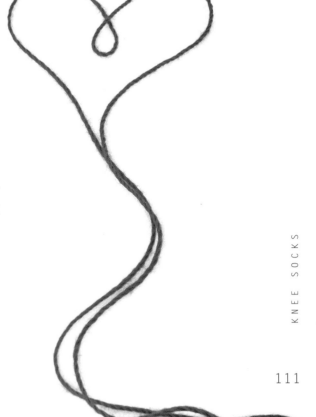

'I DON'T KNOW HOW I MAKE THE MOST ROTTEN BOBBLE, I JUST HAVE A TALENT FOR IT. IT'S JUST NOT MY THING. BUT KNITTING - I CAN KNIT YOU ANYTHING. I MAKE SURE TO ALWAYS READ THE PATTERN THROUGH TWO OR THREE TIMES BEFORE I START. IT'S JUST ONE OF THOSE THINGS I ALWAYS DO AND I ALWAYS CHECK THE ROWS THAT I'VE KNITTED BEFORE I START THE NEXT ONE – SAVES A LOT OF HEARTACHE LATER ON!'
BUNNY REES

BALACLAVA

The balaclava is not for the faint-hearted! It always demands the question – 'Who is under there'? Originally conceived as a catwalk piece, complete with superhero eye stripe and proportionally large bobble, there's no blending into the crowd with this design. Feel the power of anonymity surround you – you no longer need to be yourself, you can be anyone. Wear it loud and proud!

MEASUREMENTS

39cm from bottom edge to crown

23.5cm wide, sewn up

YARN

250g DK yarn, 1 strand, 180g in grey (MC) and 70g in black (CC)

TENSION

10cm square in stocking stitch: 18 sts x 24 rows

NEEDLES AND NOTIONS

5mm knitting needles

4mm knitting needles (optional for firmer rib)

Tapestry needle

STITCHES AND TECHNIQUES

2 x 2 rib

Stocking stitch

Moss stitch

Cable cast-on method

Card for pompom template

NOTES

(L) Left side of mouth and eye panels

(R) Right side of mouth and eye panels

INSTRUCTIONS

Using MC, cast on 89 sts, leaving long end of yarn for sewing up.

2 x 2 rib

Row 1: *K2, P2, repeat from * to last st, K1.

Row 2: P1, *K2, P2, repeat from * to end.

Repeat these 2 rows until 34 rows are completed.

Work 10 rows in st st.

Mouth panel

Row 45: K40, [P1, K1] 4 times, P1, K to end.

Row 46: P39, [K1, P1] 5 times, K1, P to end.

Row 47: K38, [P1, K1] 6 times, P1, K to end.

Mouth opening

Row 48 (WS): P37, [K1, P1] twice, cast off 7 sts in pattern, K1, P1, K1, P to end.

Row 49 (R): K37, [K1, P1] twice, turn and work on right-hand side only.

Row 50 (R): [P1, K1] twice, P to end.

Row 51 (R): K37, [K1, P1] twice.

Cut off yarn leaving about 8cm for sewing up.

Rejoin yarn to sts on left-hand needle and work as follows:

Row 49 (L): [P1, K1] twice, K to end.

Row 50 (L): P37, [K1, P1] twice.

Row 51 (L): [P1, K1] twice, K to end.

Row 52 (WS): P37, [K1, P1] twice, turn, cast on 7 sts using cable cast-on method, turn and work across sts on left-hand needle: [P1, K1] twice, P to end.

Row 53: As row 47.

Row 54: As row 46.

Row 55: As row 45.

Row 56: Purl to end.

Continue in st st across all sts for a further 2 rows.

Eye panel

Change to CC and work 2 rows in st st.

Row 61: K30, [P1, K1] 14 times, P1, K to end.

Row 62: P29, [K1, P1] 15 times, K1, P to end.

Row 63: K28, [P1, K1] 16 times, P1, K to end.

Row 64 (WS): P28, [P1, K1] twice, cast off 25 sts in pattern, P1, K1, P1, P to end. Mark centre st of cast off.

Row 65 (R): Working on right-hand side sts, K28, [P1, K1] twice.

Row 66 (R): [K1, P1] twice, P to end.

Row 67 (R): K28, [P1, K1] twice.

Cut off yarn leaving about 8cm for sewing up.

Return to second set of sts, rejoin yarn and work as follows:

Row 65 (L): [K1, P1] twice, K to end.

Row 66 (L): P28, [P1, K1] twice.

Row 67 (L): [K1, P1] twice, K to end.

Row 68 (WS): P28, [P1, K1] twice, turn work.

Cast on 10 sts, turn and pick up 5 sts from cast off edge with left-hand needle using marked stitch as centre guide, work as follows: [P1, K1] twice, P1.

Turn and cast on 10 sts, turn, now work across sts on left-hand needle: [K1, P1] twice, P to end.

Row 69: As row 63.

Row 70: As row 62.

Row 71: As row 61.

Row 72: P.

Break off yarn leaving long end for sewing up.

Using MC, work 16 rows in st st (ending at row 88).

Crown decrease

Row 89: *K6, K2tog, repeat from * to last st, K1.

Row 90 and all alternate rows: P.

Row 91: *K5, K2tog, repeat from * to last st, K1.

Row 93: *K4, K2tog, repeat from * to last st, K1.

Row 95: *K3, K2tog, repeat from * to last st, K1.

Row 97: *K2, K2tog, repeat from * to last st, K1.

Row 99: *K1, K2tog, repeat from * to last st, K1.

Row 101: K2tog to last st, K1.

Row 102: P2tog to end. 6 sts.

TO MAKE UP

Cut off the yarn, leaving a long end. Using a tapestry needle, thread the yarn through the remaining sts and pull tightly, avoiding puckering. Sew in the end, securing the sts.

Taking care to match the colour changes, join the sides together from the bottom of the rib to the end of the crown. Sew in the loose ends neatly around the mouth and eye holes.

Make a pompom in the contrast colour yarn, using a template 10cm in diameter with a 2.5cm hole. Tie the centre tightly and fasten it on top of the hat.

'THE NORTH CIRCULAR RAINBOW BALACLAVA SHOULD BE MANDATORY UNIFORM FOR ALL THE ARMIES OF THE WORLD. THAT AND NOTHING ELSE...NOW IF I COULD JUST GET ONE OF THEIR KNITTING GRANDMAS TO KNIT ME A SONG.'
ANTHONY KIEDIS, RED HOT CHILI PEPPERS

KNIGHT'S HOOD

This slouchy hood with bouncy ribbing slips on over the head. Hide away with it over your head or wear it back as a hood over your coat.

MEASUREMENTS

38cm long x 26cm wide, sewn up

YARN

250g DK yarn, 2 strands together

TENSION

10cm square in 2 x 2 rib, measured relaxed: 22 sts x 19 rows

NEEDLES AND NOTIONS

6mm knitting needles
Tapestry needle

STITCHES AND TECHNIQUES

2 x 2 rib

INSTRUCTIONS

Cast on 90 sts, leaving long end of yarn for sewing up.

2 x 2 rib

Row 1: *K2, P2, repeat from * to last 2 sts, K2.
Row 2: *P2, K2, repeat from * to last 2 sts, P2.
Repeat rows 1 and 2 until 32 rows are completed, dec 1 st every 4th row on left-hand edge only (first dec row 3; last dec row 31). 82 sts.

Shape hood

Continue working in 2 x 2 rib.
With RS facing, and counting the next row as row 1, dec 1 st at right-hand edge only on rows 1, 4, 7, 9, 11, 12, 13, 14, 15, 16, 17, 18. 70 sts.
Counting next row as row 1 again, inc 1 st at same edge on rows 1, 2, 3, 4, 5, 6, 7, 8, 10, 12, 15, 18. 82 sts. Hood shaping completed.
Counting next row as row 1, continue in 2 x 2 rib on these sts for further 32 rows, inc 1 st every 4th row on left-hand edge only (first inc row 3; last inc row 31). 90 sts. Cast off loosely in rib or using crochet hook method.

TO MAKE UP

Fold the hood in half, along the rib, matching up the cast-on and cast-off edges. Stitch the hood's curve together, starting at the top, and continue stitching down to the cast-on and cast-off edges. Turn the work sideways, for it will have the rib running horizontally when on, with the curve at the top. Create the neck join by sewing the cast-on and cast-off edges together at the bottom of the hood for about 12cm. Sew in the loose ends.

NARWHAL BLANKET

The magical unicorn horns of antiquity held inspiring awe and wonder, we now know to be of the magnificent narwhal whale. Just one of the many species at threat from loss of habitat in the Arctic. The mesmerizing lines of cabling of this luxurious throw evoke the waves of the icy oceans that narwhals dive beneath while we snuggle under it, dreaming by the fire.

MEASUREMENTS
184cm long x 140cm wide

YARN
1500g DK yarn, 1 strand

TENSION
10cm square in stocking stitch: 20 sts x 24 rows

NEEDLES AND NOTIONS
4mm knitting needles
Cable needle
Tapestry needle

STITCHES AND TECHNIQUES
2 x 2 rib
Cabling

NOTES
This blanket is knitted in four panels that are sewn together later.

INSTRUCTIONS

Right edge panel
Cast on 111 sts and start in 2 x 2 rib as follows:
Row 1: K1, *P2, K2, repeat from* to last 2 sts, P2.
Row 2: *K2, P2 repeat from * to last 3 sts, K2, P1.
Repeat rows 1 and 2 for 8cm.
Work travelling cable pattern as follows:
Row 1: K1, P2, [K2, P2] 4 times, [(K6, P2) twice, (K2, P2) twice] 3 times, (K6, P2) twice, K2, P2.
Row 2 and all alternate rows: K knit sts and P purl sts.
Row 3: K1, P2, [K2, P2] 4 times, [C6F, P2, C6B, P2, (K2, P2) twice] 3 times, C6F, P2, C6B, P2, K2, P2.
Row 5: As row 1.
Row 6: As row 2.
Repeat these 6 rows twice more. 18 rows completed.
Row 19: K1, P2, [K2, P2] 3 times, K6, [P2, (K2, P2) twice, K6, P2, K6] 3 times, P2, [K2, P2] twice, K6, P2.
Row 21: K1, P2, [K2, P2] 3 times, C6B, [P2, (K2, P2) twice, C6F, P2, C6B] 3 times, P2, [K2, P2] twice, C6F, P2.
Row 23: As row 19.
Row 24: As row 2.
Repeat rows 19–24 twice more. 36 rows completed.
Repeat these 36 rows until work measures about 176cm.
Work 8cm of 2 x 2 rib as at beginning of panel. Cast off loosely in rib or using crochet cast-off method.

Left edge panel

Cast on 111 sts and start in 2 x 2 rib as follows:

Row 1: *P2, K2, repeat from * to last 3 sts, P2, K1.

Row 2: P1, *K2, P2, repeat from * to last 2 sts, K2.

Repeat rows 1 and 2 for 8cm.

Work travelling cable pattern as follows:

Row 1: P2, K2, P2, [(K6, P2) twice, (K2, P2) twice] 4 times, [K2, P2] twice, K1.

Row 2 and all alternate rows: K knit sts and P purl sts.

Row 3: P2, K2, P2, [C6F, P2, C6B, P2, (K2, P2) twice] 4 times, [K2, P2] twice, K1.

Row 5: As row 1.

Row 6: As row 2.

Repeat these 6 rows twice more. 18 rows completed.

Row 19: P2, K6, [P2, (K2, P2) twice, K6, P2, K6] 3 times, P2, [K2, P2] twice, K6, P2, [K2, P2] 3 times, K1.

Row 21: P2, C6B, [P2, (K2, P2) twice, C6F, P2, C6B] 3 times, P2, [K2, P2] twice, C6F, P2 [K2, P2] 3 times, K1.

Row 23: As row 19.

Row 24: As row 2.

Repeat rows 19–24 twice more. 36 rows completed.

Repeat these 36 rows until work measures about 176cm.

Work 8cm of 2 x 2 rib as at beginning of panel. Cast off as for right edge panel.

Middle panel (Make 2)

Cast on 98 sts and start in 2 x 2 rib as follows:

Row 1: P2, *K2, P2, repeat from * to end.

Row 2: *K2, P2, repeat from * to last 2 sts, K2.

Repeat rows 1 and 2 for 8cm.

Work travelling cable pattern as follows:

Row 1: P2, K2, P2, [(K6, P2) twice, (K2, P2) twice] 3 times, (K6, P2) twice, K2, P2.

Row 2 and all alternate rows: K knit sts and P purl sts.

Row 3: P2, K2, P2, [C6F, P2, C6B, P2, (K2, P2) twice] 3 times, C6F, P2, C6B, P2, K2, P2.

Row 5: As row 1.

Row 6: As row 2.

Repeat these 6 rows twice more. 18 rows completed.

Row 19: P2, K6, [P2, (K2, P2) twice, K6, P2, K6] 3 times, P2, [K2, P2] twice, K6, P2.

Row 21: P2, C6B, [P2, (K2, P2) twice, C6F, P2, C6B] 3 times, P2, [K2, P2] twice, C6F, P2.

Row 23: As row 19.

Row 24: As row 2.

Repeat rows 19–24 twice more. 36 rows completed.

Repeat these 36 rows until work measures about 176cm.

Work 8cm of 2 x 2 rib as at beginning of panel. Cast off as for right edge panel.

TO MAKE UP

Keeping the rib along the edges, sew the four panels together. Sew in the loose ends.

KNITTING KNOW HOW

YARN CHOICE

Since Stone Age times the tangled web of animal fibres has been drawn out, twisting and teasing to form a continuous thread. In England, the woollen thread runs back all the way to our earliest recorded history – Roman emperors cherished British woollen cloth so fine it was 'comparable with a spider's web'.

We believe in pure natural fibres (with no synthetic blends) using a 'cradle to cradle' approach, meaning that these pure yarns can go back to the soil at the end of their natural life cycle – from the grass eaten by sheep and around again into wool proteins growing in the sun on a sheep's back. This sustainable process creates a fibre that is practical in its natural form, a fantastic insulator able to stay warm even when wet, flame retardant and naturally elastic so it holds it's shape for a long lifespan.

Our favourite British yarns are from the alpaca (which is also naturally hypoallergenic!), sheep's wool from Blue-faced Leicester and Wensleydale (the ringletted sheep famed for having no kemp in their wool) and British cashmere from the only remaining commercial herd of cashmere goats in England. These are the kings of British fibres for softness.

It all begins with a single strand, knitted up to your own creation. We use 100% British wool and also source from other great British suppliers. We look for yarns that have every part of the process done locally – carding, spinning and dying – endorsing the best ecological solutions available and supporting the move towards better and better transparency with our custom.

So where can you find good yarns? We would love you to use our ethos to look for the finest fibres from the best-treated animals in your locality so you can support your own area. If you find yarn you like, ask who produces it – maybe it's your local knitting shop or a farm nearby that's spinning its own.

When a yarn has lost its shop label, it can be hard to know what weight of yarn you have in your hand. A simple trick to help you decide is to measure the 'wraps per centimetre'. Carefully wrapping the yarn around a ruler, lying each strand closely next to the previous one so that you cannot see the ruler through the yarn. When you reach 2.5cm, count the number of strands used. For the yarns used in this book, Aran is around 9 wraps, DK is around 10–11 wraps and 4 ply is 12–13 wraps per centimetre.

WASH CARE

Careless washing has been the downfall of many a fine knit. Even in the machine-washable and synthetic fibre age, many a hasty wash can result in shrunken felted knits. The following simple rules will help you to keep your knits ship shape.

Lay out a towel and place your garment on it. Using pins that won't rust, pin a rough outline shape of your knitwear onto the towel. This forms a guide for getting your knit back to the right shape after washing.

Using warm water (suitable for bare hands) with a liquid wool wash well diluted in the water, squeeze the knit to get the water swooshing in and out of the fabric. Never rub the knit as this can felt the yarn. Then rinse the garment very well to remove all the soap.

To dry, tie the garment securely in a cotton wash bag and spin it in the washing machine or roll the knit up in a dry towel and squeeze out the excess moisture. Then lay the garment back on the towel and gently push it into shape to the outline of the pins. Leave the garment flat on the towel to dry completely.

RECYCLING YARN

Once your knitwear tires out, you can bring it back to life by unravelling and re-knitting your yarn.

Take your tired old knit and carefully unpick all seams. At the cast-off edge, find the end of the yarn (you may need to make a brave snip) and gently unravel the knitting. Once you get going, you can whizz along very satisfyingly, winding the yarn around a large old book as you go to create a hank.

Tie the hank loosely with short lengths of the same yarn to keep it together and then slide it off the book. Wash the hank in lukewarm water, gently squeezing out the excess. Lightly steam the yarn to fluff up the fibres and hang the hank on a washing line to dry, with a weight attached to help take out any crinkles.

Once the yarn is dry, get an unsuspecting person to hold the hank taut in both hands while you tell really raucous stories as you wind the yarn loosely back into a ball. Start by wrapping the yarn loosely around your fingers until your fingers are full. Then pinch and twist the yarn into a figure of eight, fold it in half, then continue gently wrapping the yarn, turning it slightly to create a round ball and – bingo! – you are ready to knit again.

Compost

Using the 'cradle to cradle' inspired approach, we recommend that your natural yarns should eventually, after a useful long life cycle, go back to the earth. Chopped up into small pieces and added gradually to the heap, pure wool is a great addition to compost as it has the ability to hold water and slowly release nutrients back into the soil.

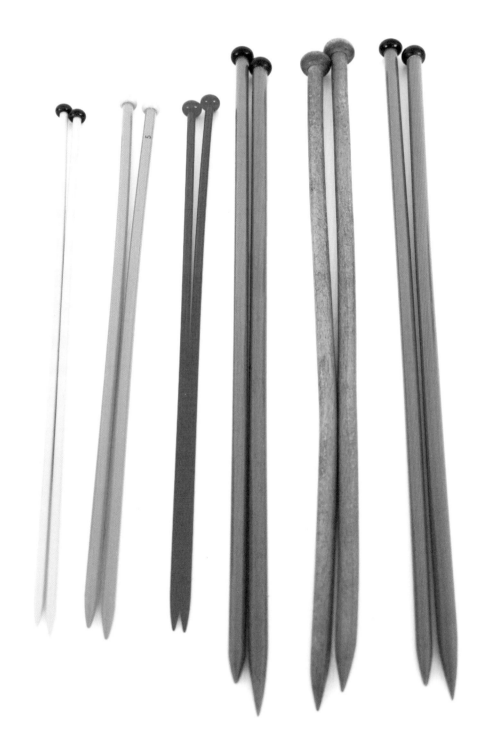

ABBREVIATIONS

[ ] – repeat instructions between these markings specified number of times

MC – main colour

CC – contrast colour

DPNs – double-pointed needles

CN – cable needle

PM – place marker

RS – right side

WS – wrong side

st(s) – stitch(es)

dec – decrease/decreasing

inc – increase/increasing

K – knit stitch

P – purl stitch

KB1 – knit 1 through back of stitch

PB1 – purl 1 through back of stitch

st st – stocking stitch

K2tog – knit 2 stitches together

K3tog – knit 3 stitches together

P2tog – purl 2 stitches together

PB2tog – purl 2 stitches together through back of stitches

sl1 – slip 1 stitch without knitting it

sl1-k1-psso – slip stitch, knit next stitch, pass slipped stitch over knitted stitch

sl2tog-k1-psso – slip 2 stitches together to right-hand needle, knit next stitch, pass 2 slipped stitches over knitted stitch

M1 – make 1 stitch by lifting horizontal strand between stitches and knitting into back of it

yo – yarn over needle

wyf – with yarn forward

C4B – (cable 4 back) slip 2 stitches to cable needle, leave at back of work, knit 2 from left-hand needle, then knit 2 from cable needle

C4F – (cable 4 front) slip 2 stitches to cable needle, leave at front of work, knit 2 from left-hand needle, then knit 2 from cable needle

C6B – slip 3 stitches to cable needle, leave at back of work, knit 3 from left-hand needle, then knit 3 from cable needle

C6F – slip 3 stitches to cable needle, leave at front of work, knit 3 from left-hand needle, then knit 3 from cable needle

C8B – slip 4 stitches to cable needle, leave at back of work, knit 4 from left-hand needle, then knit 4 from cable needle

C8F – slip 4 stitches to cable needle, leave at front of work, knit 4 from left-hand needle, then knit 4 from cable needle

C12B – slip 6 stitches to cable needle, leave at back of work, knit 2, purl 2, knit 2 from left-hand needle, then knit 2, purl 2, knit 2 from cable needle

C12F – slip 6 stitches to cable needle, leave at back of work, knit 2, purl 2, knit 2 from left-hand needle, then knit 2, purl 2, knit 2 from cable needle

T3B – (twist 3 back) slip next stitch to cable needle, leave at back of work, knit 2 from left-hand needle, then knit 1 (or purl 1 as appropriate for moss stitch) from cable needle

T3F – (twist 3 front) slip 2 stitches to cable needle, leave at front of work, knit 1 (or purl 1 as appropriate for moss stitch) from left-hand needle, then knit 2 from cable needle

T5B – slip 2 stitches to cable needle, leave at back of work, knit 3 from left-hand needle, then purl 2 from cable needle

T5F – slip 3 stitches to cable needle, leave at front of work, purl 2 from left-hand needle, then knit 3 from cable needle

C5B/C5F – (cross 5 back/front) slip 3 stitches to cable needle, leave at back (or front) of work, knit 2 from left-hand needle, slip 1 stitch from left point of cable needle back to left-hand needle and purl it, then knit 2 from cable needle

'EVERYONE SHOULD GIVE KNITTING A TRY, JUST BE SURE TO START WITH SOMETHING SIMPLE SO YOU DON'T GET PUT OFF. ONCE YOU GET THE HANG OF IT, IT IS VERY THERAPUTIC.'
Aileen Barr

KNITTING TECHNIQUES

CASTING ON
There are many different methods of casting on, each suitable to different types of stitches. Some give a firm edge, others a softer, more stretchy edge. Whichever cast you choose, you should try not to make it too tight, as it's less comfortable to wear and the yarn will wear out more quickly.

Cable cast-on method
The method we use is cable cast on, a strong but flexible cast-on method using two needles.

Step 1
Make a slipknot on the left-hand needle and insert your right-hand needle through it as if to knit.

Step 2
Knit a stitch and place it on the left-hand needle.

Step 3
Insert the right-hand needle between the last two stitches. Knit a stitch and place it on the left-hand needle. Continue in this manner, repeating Step 3 until you have the desired number of stitches.

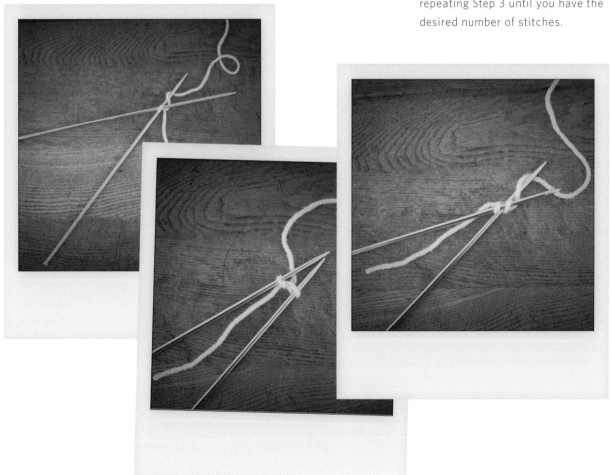

CASTING OFF

Casting off secures the last row of stitches so they don't unravel. Try not to pull your working yarn too tight, so the edge remains stretchy.

Cast off using needles
Step 1

Knit the first two stitches. With the left-hand needle bring the first stitch over the second stitch and slip it off the needle. One stitch remains on the right-hand needle.

Step 2

Knit another stitch, then bring the first stitch over the second stitch and slip it off the needle, as before. Continue in this manner, repeating Step 2 until one loop remains. Cut the yarn and thread it through the remaiining stitch, then pull tight to secure it.

Casting off using a crochet hook

A crochet hook cast off ensures a flexible edge on ribbed knits. Always knit the last row loosely or with needles one size larger.

Step 1

Take the needle out and reinsert it through the stitches, so that the yarn is on the opposite side of the needle.

Step 2

Using a crochet hook, cast off from right to left, slipping stitch through stitch across the row without using extra yarn. Pull the yarn through the last stitch to secure it.

1. Mattress stitch

One of the simplest way of joining work is mattress stitch. To join, place the two pieces together with the right sides facing you. Seam from side to side, going under the horizontal bar between the stitches, one stitch in from the edge as shown.

2. Flat seam

This method of joining seams results in a flatter, almost invisible seam, which is suitable for smaller knits, such as gloves. To join, place the work together with the right sides facing up. Seam side to side, picking up the 'head' of each stitch from alternate sides.

For a more pronounced, firmer edge, knit the first and last stitch of each pattern row, creating 'heads' of stiches exposed as stitch 'bumps', which can lock together easily.

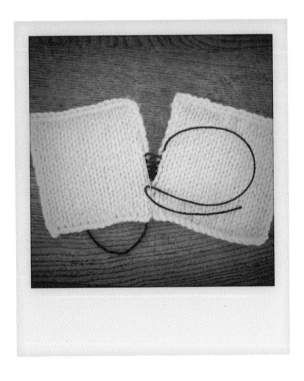

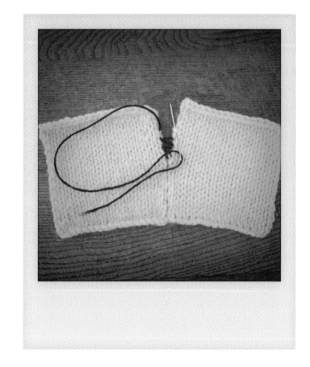

MEASURING TENSION

Tension, or gauge, in knitting refers to the number of stitches across and down per square centimetre of knitted fabric. The tension knitted can result in widely different sized garments, so check your tension to ensure your knitting will come out the right size.

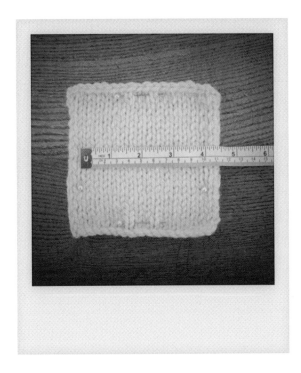

Even if you use the same yarn, you will get more stitches per centimeter using a smaller needle than you will using a larger needle. So any project you knit will only have the correct measurements if your tension is correct, even if you use the size of needles and thickness of yarn specified in the instructions. You may be a tight knitter or a loose knitter, and you have to allow for this by changing your needle size to get the correct tension.

Before you begin your garment, make a test swatch of at least 10cm square, which should be big enough for you to measure it. Using pins and a tape measure, place two pins in the swatch to measure 10cm. Then count how many stitches are between the pins. Repeat to count how many rows there are in 10cm.

If the number of stitches and rows does not correspond with the tension given in the pattern, you must change the needle size. To get fewer stitches to the centimeter, use a larger needle and to get more stitches, use a smaller needle. Continue to try different needle sizes until you get the required tension.

'YOU KNOW THE REAL ART OF HAND KNITTING IS DOWN TO BEING SPOT ON WITH YOUR TENSION. THE TENSION SWATCH TELLS YOU HOW TO ADJUST IT TO THE SIZE OF GARMENT AND IF YOU'RE GETTING IT RIGHT. RUSH PAST THE TENSION MEASUREMENT AND YOU CAN SPEND A LOT OF TIME CURSING WHILE YOU UNPICK!'
GRAN EILEEN

✥ 'LOOK AT THE EDGE OF A PIECE OF KNITTING - STOCKING STITCH,
GARTER STITCH OR A PATTERNED PIECE, YOU WILL SEE THE STITCHES
ALONG THE EDGE CAN BEST BE DESCRIBED AS 'DOT' AND 'DASH'. WHEN
SEWING TWO PIECES OF KNITTING TOGETHER IT IS IMPORTANT TO MATCH
A DOT STITCH ON ONE PIECE WITH A DASH STITCH ON THE OTHER PIECE.
WHEN STARTING A PIECE OF KNITTING FROM A PATTERN WITH A RIB
EDGE, I MAKE SURE THE NUMBER OF STITCHES AND THE SUBSEQUENT RIB
KNITTED WILL ALLOW FOR A 'THIS' SEAM, I.E. K2, P2 RIB SHOULD END
K1, AND THE FOLLOWING ROW START P1, K2, P2 ETC; LIKEWISE K1, P1
RIB SHOULD END K1 AND THE FOLLOWING ROW START, AND END, P1. THE
EXTRA, OR LESSER, STITCH SHOULD BE TAKEN INTO ACCOUNT WHEN
FOLLOWING A PATTERN THAT HAS NOT ALLOWED FOR THIS BY M1 OR K2TOG
ON THE FIRST ROW AFTER FINISHING THE RIBBING. BY FOLLOWING THIS
METHOD THE RIBBING ENDS UP CONTINUOUSLY ALL ROUND WITHOUT A
BREAK FOR SEAMS.

SO, ASSUMING CASTING ON HAS BEEN CARRIED OUT WITH A SLIP STITCH
AND THE CABLE METHOD, UNDO ONE LOOP ON THE SLIP STITCH AT THE
BEGINNING OF THE CAST-ON. PLACE THE TWO PIECES OF KNITTING RIGHT
SIDES TOGETHER - THE PIECE WITH THE SEWING-UP THREAD NEAREST
YOU. THE FIRST STITCH ON THE OPPOSITE PIECE IS THE SMALL LOOP
SEEMINGLY BEHIND THE FIRST CAST-ON STITCH. PUSH THE NEEDLE
THROUGH FROM RIGHT SIDE TO WRONG SIDE, THE NEXT STITCH SHOULD BE
BACK THROUGH THE 'DOT' FIRST CAST-ON STITCH AND ACROSS THROUGH
THE 'DASH', WHICH IS NEXT IN LINE ON THE PIECE NEAREST YOU, BACK
THROUGH THE NEXT 'DOT' AND ACROSS TO THE OPPOSITE `DASH', AND SO
ON UNTIL THE SEAM IS COMPLETE. STRAIGHT STITCHING, UNTIL THE END
OF THE SEAM IS REACHED, THEN BACK STITCH ONCE OR TWICE AND SEW
THE END OF THE YARN BACK ALONG THE SEAM.'
SHIRLEY

139

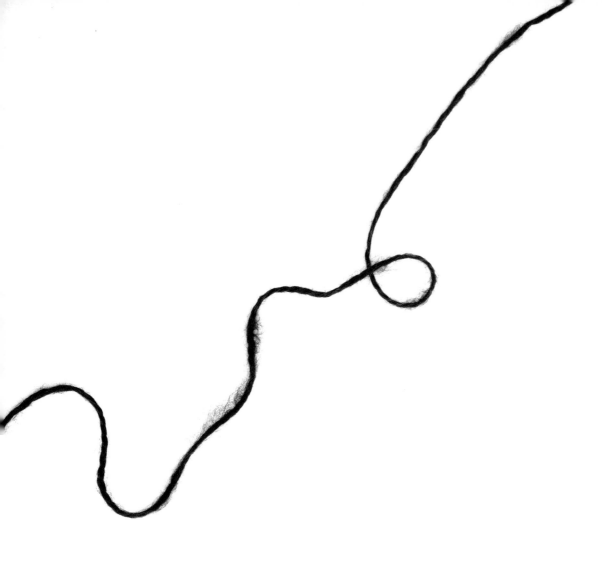

'THE FIRST STEP TO SUSTAINABLE FASHION IS
UNDERSTANDING THE PROCESS OF MAKING! *A GOOD YARN*
NOT ONLY ACHIEVES THIS BUT ITS CLEAR GUIDELINES
HELP YOU TO TAP INTO YOUR INNER CREATIVITY AND
LEARN ABOUT THE MAKING OF MAKING! KNIT ON!'
DAVID DE ROTHSCHILD - ECO ACTIVIST AND EXPLORER

ACKNOWLEDGEMENTS

First we would like to thank our wonderful publisher Kyle Books and designer Georgia Vaux for her brilliant intuitive work.

The patterns in this book are the result of teamwork over the last few years. We owe a lot to the perfectionism and meticulous attention to detail of Hania Dudziak, also to the invaluable wisdom of Shirley Hunt, Patricia Sumner and Anna Maltz. This book would never have been possible without their knitting talent and drive. A huge thanks to our supportive, hardworking knitters and pattern checkers Carole, Ann, Jen, Chris, Susan, 'Bunny', Aileen, Lorraine, Beryl, Janet and Sheila, aka 'Knit and Purl'. We cannot thank you enough.

Thank you to the eyes behind the lens, our talented photographers and dear friends: the incredible James 'Mori' Moriarty, the beautiful Katie Tomlinson, the visionary Lyle Owerko and the magic-capturing Emir Eralp, Roo Kendall and Christina Smith.

Thanks to our models: Zoe Havler, for bleaching your hair to death at the right moment, Aynzli Jones, ever the joker, Hannah Janes, Vicky 'toothbrush' Murdoch, for your contagious Scottish laughter and finally Baby Buddy Blue, for braving the balaclava shot.

To Sarah and Paula at Storm models, gratitude for all your belief in nurturing our talent from the very start.

A double air kiss thank you to our fashion creatives, Deep Kailey, Jess Bumpus, Amber Valletta, Attienna Roilett and our rock and friend Niamh Quinn. Special thanks goes to Lester Dales for his mirth and clever maths and to Susanne Tidefreighter for all her kindness and business wisdom. Final thanks goes to my very own gran, Eileen.

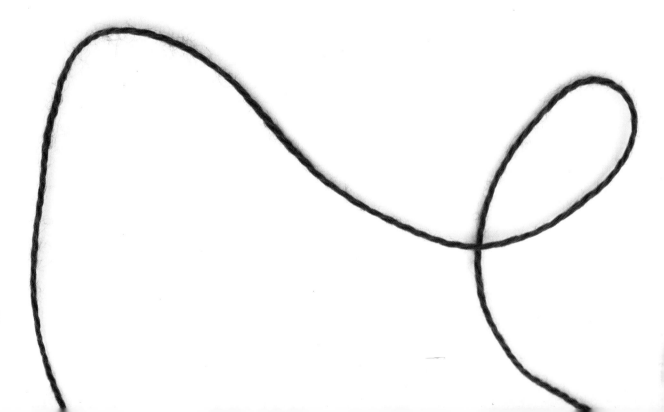

First published in Great Britain in 2014 by
Kyle Books, an imprint of Kyle Cathie Ltd
192-198 Vauxhall Bridge Road
London SW1V 1DX
general.enquiries@kylebooks.com
www.kylebooks.com

Printer line 10 9 8 7 6 5 4 3 2 1

ISBN 978 0 85783 224 5

Project Editor: Judith Hannam
Editorial Assistant: Claire Rogers
Copy Editor: Karen Hemmingway
Designer: Georgia Vaux
Photographers: James Moriarty, Christina Smith, Emir Eralp, Hayley
Brown, Katie Tomlinson, Lyle Owerko, Roo Kendall
Production: Nic Jones, Gemma John and Lisa Pinnell

A Cataloguing in Publication record for this title is available from
the British Library.

Colour reproduction by ALTA London
Printed and bound in China by Toppan Leefung Printing Ltd

A GOOD YARN